Early Childhood Number Games

Teachers Reinvent Math Instruction
Pre-K through Third Grade

Alice P. Wakefield
Old Dominion University

Foreword by Constance Kamii

Allyn and Bacon
Boston London Toronto Sydney Tokyo Singapore

To my family . . .

For their abiding
encouragement and
loving support

Illustrations: **Courtney Waterfield Saintsing**
Graphic Art: **Debby Miller**

Copyright © 1998 by Allyn & Bacon
A Viacom Company
160 Gould Street
Needham Heights, Massachusetts 02194-2130

Internet: www.abacon.com
America Online: keyword: College Online

Library of Congress Cataloging-in-Publication Data

Wakefield, Ali.
    Early childhood number games : teachers reinvent math instruction,
preK through 3rd grade / Alice P. Wakefield ; foreword by Constance
Kamii.
        p.   cm.
    Includes bibliographical references (p.   -   ) and index.
    ISBN 0-205-19566-0
    1. Arithmetic--Study and teaching (Early childhood) 2. Number
concept--Study and teaching (Early childhood) 3. Games in
mathematics education.   I. Title.
QA135.5.W245 1997
372.7'2044--dc21
                                           97-42882
                                           CIP

Printed in the United States of America
10 9 8 7 6 5 4 3 2 1   02 01 00 99 98 97

Table of Contents

Foreword

This is an excellent collection of math games invented by teachers and tested by them in their own classrooms. Alice Wakefield worked closely with them, and I have personally seen their excitement and enthusiasm for these games. I described many games in <u>Young Children Reinvent Arithmetic</u>, <u>Young Children Continue to Reinvent Arithmetic 2nd Grade</u>, and <u>Young Children Continue to Reinvent Arithmetic, 3rd Grade</u>, but teachers are always looking for more. I can now refer them to this book.

A strength of this book is that the games are easy to find (because each one is on a separate page), and the first line immediately tells the reader what it is good for (such as "addends 4 through 10"). I like the variety as well as the different versions of the same game.

I hope the reader will take time to read the text, too, because how we use games makes an enormous difference to what children get out of playing them. Wakefield gives short and readable pointers about assessment, what to do or not to do with children who count-all, noise in the classroom, and so on. Her recommendations are theoretically sound and practical.

I would like to emphasize a few points Wakefield made. First, games are only part of a constructivist mathematics program. The two other types of activities I advocate are (a) discussions of the different procedures students invented to solve "word" problems and (b) the use of situations in daily living such as taking attendance and collecting money for a field trip. Games do not challenge children to logico-arithmetize contents. For example, if a child has $5 and buys two bags of chips at 69 cents each and three cans of pop at 45 cents each, s/he has to logico-arithmetize these contents to know how much money will be left.

My last comment is about the inseparability of our intellectual goals and socio-moral goals for children. At a time when we are beset by drug problems, violence, teenage pregnancies, etc., it is important to remember that socio-moral education goes on during every moment of the school day even if we do not think

---

about it. If we use worksheets to drill children on rules they do not understand, we unwittingly reinforce blind obedience and conformity to rules that do not make sense to them. If, on the other hand, we use games and encourage independent, critical thinking and debate, we are likely to get children who can make decisions for themselves by considering all the relevant factors. The moral fortitude necessary to say "No" to temptations can come only from personal conviction about what is right in specific situations. Games are fun, but, in the hands of teachers who know how to use them well, they are also good for children's socio-moral development.

Constance Kamii

Acknowledgments

This book could not have been written if I had not attended three summer seminars with Constance Kamii at the University of Alabama-Birmingham. I am indebted to her for her guidance and patience as I build a clearer understanding for Piaget's theory on the construction of knowledge. She continues to challenge and inspire me to learn more. I am thankful to her for reading this manuscript and telling me what she honestly thought about each chapter. It is a better book because of her thought-provoking critique.

Additionally, I am grateful for the contributions made by the many classroom teachers who have taken my class on Integrating Math Into the Early Childhood Curriculum. Many of these teachers were chugging along, vaguely dissatisfied, but trying to implement the math curriculums approved by their various school districts. Their commitment and determination to stand up for what is in the best interest of children has been both gratifying and inspiring to observe. A special thank you is due one group of teachers in Gloucester County, Virginia who met with me for independent study several years ago. Together we learned that math games were not only good for children, they were good for teachers as well. As their students "reinvented" arithmetic, the teachers own understanding for math instruction was transformed. For children to form logico-mathematical understanding, teachers must "reinvent" their math instruction. This book tells the story of this process.

I am indebted to my illustrator. I first met Courtney Waterfield Saintsing when she enrolled in my math class. The games she developed and shared with us in class were imaginatively designed and beautifully rendered. I was delighted when she agreed to illustrate this book. What a bonus it was to work with an illustrator with a constructivist philosophy.

To all the pre-service and in-service teachers who thought of games described in this collection, I am most thankful. Their ideas will enliven many a math lesson for young children and help their teachers to present math in a new way.

Introduction

It is my hope that this book will help teachers move toward establishing classroom environments which encourage and support collaborative problem solving, invention and thinking. Games require high levels of mental and social involvement. It is active involvement such as this that makes game playing a great first step to moving away from the drill-and-practice, silent-classroom mentality we endured when we were learning about numbers. Happily, there are teachers all over the country who, on their own initiative, are finding ways to encourage math thinking and social interaction in their classrooms. This book is full of stories about the successes and frustrations of teachers I know who began to change their math instruction by introducing number-game play.

There are other teachers who are being encouraged by their supervisors to use manipulatives as a first step to changing the way they teach math. School districts throughout the country are purchasing elaborate and expensive manipulative materials for their primary teachers. I have seen how some of this material is being used, and it worries me. I watched a first-grade teacher use manipulative materials to teach her students about place value and regrouping. The children were busy representing with chips the numbers called out by their teacher. Whenever the children collected a tenth chip, the ten chips were gathered together and placed in a cupcake paper. To represent that the ten "ones" had been miraculously transformed into one "ten," the children moved their collected chips to the left side of their desk under the label "*tens*." I intentionally use the word "miraculous" here, because that is what some of the children thought happened! This is an example of what Marilyn Burns (1994) refers to as the "mysterious and often magical rules and procedures that children must practice." This exercise was no more than the same old rote math activity, now practiced in three dimensions instead of two. The sad truth is that exercises such as this one are often wrongly described as the positive change of more "hands-on" representation called for by the new NCTM Standards.

Now, wait a minute, you say. Surely all manipulation is not so bad as this example. So, what makes for "good" manipulation? And, for that matter, what was so bad about this example? Very briefly put, I would say that useful manipulation is that manipulation which is driven by the student's thinking, a personal quest to figure something out. Judy decides to work on a puzzle and thinks about the placement of each piece. Jeanne counts the dots on the dice to figure out the total. Thinking drives their touch. On the other hand, "bad" manipulation is that manipulation which is driven by teacher direction as in the example above. When manipulation is used in this manner, the result is apt to be no better than a traditional worksheet, rote and tedious. However, when thinking drives the thinker to manipulate objects in his or her environment to figure something out, there is potential for much benefit. Teachers of young children need to grasp these differences before they use manipulatives in their classrooms. Unfortunately, many do not.

The long answer to the value of manipulation involves an examination of the nature of logico-mathematical knowledge and the way that children learn about number. For this I recommend Constance Kamii's classic series, <u>Young Children Reinvent Arithmetic</u> (1985, 1989, 1994). Chapter One of her first book (1985) helped me. Figuring out that "two" was a relationship that I could *not know empirically* (i.e., touch, see, hear, etc.), marked my first step toward becoming a constructivist teacher. What does this mean that you cannot see "two?" my students ask. You can *see* the two apples on the counter side-by-side. The apples are physically there and can be viewed, touched and eaten. However, the *number* of apples on the counter does not exist physically. You do not *see* the number. You see the apples. The number only exists in your head once you can conceptualize the meaning of two. Consider that you have an apple on a table in each of two rooms. Can you point to the "twoness?" Twoness is not a physical property of the apples. It is a relationship, a construction of the mind. Consequently, if a teacher has children counting (i.e., manipulating) physical objects (e.g., apples, chips, etc.), there is no guarantee that the children will form new logico-mathematical understanding from that experience. However, when children are motivated to figure out number relationships for themselves, they *will* construct logico-mathematical understanding. Children construct meaning about number relationships when they play games that require them to think about numbers in meaningful ways. For example, when children play War, they must determine which card is more. If they do not know, they must think of a way to figure it out. When children think about number relationships time and time again, they progressively construct a more sophisticated and more complex knowledge base. Since game play is driven by thinking and purpose, it is more likely to benefit the players than is the rote "twiddling" of physical objects. Thinking about number relationships when playing games with other children is what this book is about!

There are other ways besides playing games that teachers use to encourage the construction of logico-mathematical knowledge. I know a second-grade teacher who returned to school one Monday morning to find the class hamsters dead. The power had gone off, and the poor critters had died of exposure. The teacher told the children what had happened, then asked the children what they wanted to do about it. After a lively discussion and vote, the children decided that the class should raise the money themselves and buy two more hamsters. After doing some comparative shopping, the children found that they needed $26.27 to make their purchase. (I bet you know where this is heading.) "Now," said the teacher, "how much money must we each give to equal $26.27?" Can you feel the wheels turning? This is an example of the creative use of situations in daily living that constructivist teachers use throughout the school day. But, what if your hamsters don't die? Can your students vote to choose between two options, figure out the lunch order, attendance, or book order? How long is it until recess? How much paper is needed for each student to have 8 sheets? A school day is bursting with situations that challenge teachers and students alike to think and figure out problems together.

In addition to actual situations in daily living, teachers can use word problems which encourage problem-finding, as well as math thinking and discussion. Children can explain, compare and defend their answers during group problem-solving sessions. It should not be surprising that children who have not done many word problems are not very good at problem finding. Since children do not like to do what they are unable to do well, many teachers put off the word problems until the end of the lesson or avoid doing them all together. Because of this, teachers often do not begin their change to constructivist teaching by discussing word problems with their students. Typically, their first step begins with game play. One veteran teacher I know watched her students play math games for six weeks. She watched as their consuming interest lead them to ever more challenging and engaging problem solving. She became convinced that the mental and social engagement occurring during game play was affecting the thinking and social interaction during the rest of the school day. She was hooked. The positive student response to game playing lead this teacher to try another constructivist idea. She began letting her children "invent" their own strategies to solve math problems. Children shared their "inventions" with one another in sessions the children called "foolin' with numbers." This teacher formed a philosophy that affected classroom discipline, assessment, curriculum, as well as her role as an advocate for young children with school administrators, parents and colleagues. And, she says, after twenty-two years of teaching, she now loves to teach math. It began with game play.

CHAPTER 1

CALLING FOR A CHANGE

"If you always do what you always did, you will always get what you always got!" — Anonymous

In the hope of encouraging a positive change in the development of math curriculum, the National Council of Teachers of Mathematics (1989) has called for more problem solving, more "hands on" representation, and more reasoning in mathematics instruction. Many people credit the current broad examination and debate of mathematics instruction to the new NCTM Curriculum, Evaluation, and Teaching Standards. Some researchers and math educators are beginning to expand the idea of simply focusing on thinking to making thinking and invention an alternative to the prevalent use of memorized algorithms for teaching basic mathematical operations to elementary school children.

One such study by Narode, Board and Davenport (1993) reports that children who only use algorithms to compute math solutions lose their capacity for "flexible and creative thought." They found that, as children became locked into following the rules, they were less inclined to risk error by

doing their own thinking. The researchers believed that "the students lose conceptual knowledge in the process of gaining procedural knowledge."

Another article by Marilyn Burns (1994) states that "imposing the standard arithmetic algorithms on children is pedagogically risky." She says this method "interferes with their learning" and leads them to believe that "mathematics is a collection of mysterious and often magical rules and procedures that must be memorized and practiced." Young children become too distracted by the steps to think about the logic of what they are doing. Burns goes on to say that children learn that "getting the correct answer," logical or not, becomes their "most important goal."

Recently, an Education Week editorial by Steven Leinwand (1994), a math consultant with the Connecticut Department of Education, blasted algorithms. He said, "It's time to acknowledge that continuing to teach these skills to our students is not only

1

unnecessary, but counter-productive and downright dangerous." Leinwand despairs for the "sense of failure and the pain unnecessarily imposed on hundreds of thousands of students in the name of mastering these obsolete procedures." "We need to admit," he goes on, "that drill and practice of computational algorithms devour an incredibly large proportion of instructional time, precluding any real chance for actually applying mathematics and developing the conceptual understanding that underlies mathematical literacy." He implores educators and parents to insist on change and "build mathematics programs that engage and empower, unencumbered by the discriminatory shackles of computational algorithms."

A preliminary study I conducted recently with graduate student Courtney Waterfield suggests that teaching with algorithms profoundly affects even our brightest children. We wondered if children identified by their school system as being academically "gifted" in the specific area of mathematics would be able to put conventional algorithms aside and think divergently to solve some typical math problems or if they had lost their capacity for "flexible and creative thought," as Narode, Board and Davenport (1993) found. During their weekly session of advanced mathematics instruction, Waterfield presented 15 mathematically "gifted," fifth-grade students with several double-column multiplication problems. The children were challenged to solve the problems

any way they could with two stipulations. They were not to use previously learned algorithms, and they were to do the problems in their heads without paper and pencil. The following responses to the problem of 75 x 22 were explained to Waterfield, who recorded them. One student explained that $2x5 = 10$, $2x"7"(sic) = 140$, $"2"(sic)x5 = 100$ and $"2"(sic)x"7"(sic) = 1400$, leading her to conclude incorrectly that the solution was 1550. Eight children reasoned similarly, but expressed their equations somewhat more accurately as $2x5 = 10$, $2x"7"(sic) + "1"(sic) = 150$, $20x5 = 100$ and $20x70 = 1400$, totaling 1650. The most obvious way to move away from using the conventional algorithm pattern is by breaking the problem into two easier problems which can be figured out relatively easily without paper and pencil. Only six children did this. Four of them figured out that $75x2 = 150$ and $75x20 = 1500$, for a grand total of 1650. Another child reasoned even more efficiently that if $75x1 = 75$ and $75x10 = 750$ which totaled 825, twice that would be 1650. The last child reasoned that you can multiply "the top number" by 2 to get 150 and divide "the bottom number" by 2 to get 11 (i.e., $75 x22 = 150x11$). "Drop the zero off 150 until later" (he had figured out what we memorized as the "rule of 10"). "Now," he explained, "you just multiply the 15 by 11 which gives you 165." "Remember that zero we dropped?" he reminded. "Now, put it back to make 1650." You may need to think about this for a little while, but his algebraic reasoning is absolutely correct. As you can see, there were many levels of success with this problem. All but the first child got the correct answer. However, only six of the 15 children had a creative and efficient approach, breaking away from the ingrained, rote procedure they had been taught. It is important to ask ourselves why even our brightest math students choose NOT to "think" but resort to memorized, rote procedures to find solutions.

A study by Kamii and Lewis (1991) examined some effects of two different approaches to math instruction. They compared the thinking of 87 children in four second-grade classes. Two groups of children were taught with the traditional approach of teacher explanation of rules for how to work the problem followed by the student doing exercises to practice their new "skill." The two other classes were taught by teachers who used a constructivist approach. They allowed the children to "invent" solutions to problems. The students in these classes also played number games requiring them to use a variety of mathematical operations. Both invention and game playing actively involve the children in thinking and problem solving. Both the traditional and the constructivist-taught groups of children did well at "finding right answers," as determined by their standardized achievement test scores. However, when it came to explaining the logic of what they had done, the results

were startling! The children were interviewed and asked to represent with chips how they got their answers to the double-column addition problem of 16 + 17. Although almost all the children got the correct answer of 33, 83 percent of the constructivist-taught children correctly illustrated with the chips how they accomplished regrouping. Only 23 percent of the traditionally taught children were able to do this.

In another example, children were asked to figure out how many soup labels there would be altogether, if there are 21 children in the class and each one brings in 14 labels. Kamii and Lewis noted that this problem was similar to the type presented in fourth grade. Twenty percent of the constructivist-taught second graders and two percent of the traditionally taught children gave the correct answer with repeated addition. The researchers wanted to see how the children would do with mental arithmetic (i.e., without paper and pencil). They used an overhead projector to show the children one problem at a time for nine seconds. Forty-eight percent of the constructivist group and 12 percent of the traditional group could correctly say how much 98 + 43 was. Likewise, 60 percent vs 17 percent could say how much 3 x 31 was. Kamii and Lewis explain the superiority in the higher-order thinking of the constructivist-taught children by noting that constructivist teachers recognize that logico-mathematical knowledge consists of relationships which must be created mentally by each child. Number relationships are not "out there" in the physical world to be observed as an apple is. They must be formed internally by the thinker. Consequently, you cannot teach math to children by describing mathematical operations as if they were so many apples to touch and see. Math relationships can be constructed only by the child by thinking. Constructivist teachers prepare their classrooms to support this kind of math thinking. Over time, math "thinkers" are bound to construct more math relationships than children who mechanically (i.e., without meaningful thought) run memorized rules (i.e., algorithms) to get right answers.

Kamii makes a very strong case for replacing algorithms with thinking. In her latest book (1994), she presents convincing evidence illustrating that when children are taught algorithms, they are forced to give up their own numerical thinking. This happens because the initial inventions of children typically go from left to right. However, when learning addition, subtraction and multiplication algorithms, children are taught to approach the problem from right to left. Kamii notes that there is no compromise to working in opposite directions. Usually, children accept their teacher's way, and are prevented from developing their own method for solving the problem. Kamii also found that the meaning of number is often lost to children when they work algorithms.

For example, when children do $789 + 544$ by working from right to left, they approach the problem as if it were three columns of "ones" rather than a column of "hundreds", a column of "tens" and a column of "ones." The consequence is that children unlearn place value and are prevented from developing their number sense. Children who use their natural ability to think, figure out this problem by addressing the 100's first ($700 + 500 = 1200$). Next they address the 10's ($80 + 40 = 120$), and regroup any new 100's ($120 - 100 = 20$, $1200 + 100 = 1300$). The last step is to figure the 1's ($9 + 4 = 13$), regroup the 10's ($13 - 10 = 3$ and $10 + 20 = 30$) for a final answer of 1333. Not only are the children using and thus learning about place value, but by dealing with all the "hundreds" they are also constructing "number sense" for an approximate final answer. When traditional teachers first encounter a child explaining a problem such as this, they can't believe the complexity of the child's thinking. However, it is precisely this kind of thinking that leads the child to construct a knowledge base out of which ever more complex numerical operations can develop. When children learn to get answers with algorithms without understanding why these "tricks" work, their confidence in their own ability for problem solving is undermined. Kamii (1994) found that this was especially true for those children who were the weakest in math. A vicious and undermining cycle occurs. The use of algorithms works against meaningful problem solving, therefore the child does not understand how the "trick" works. This leads to lowered confidence in him or herself and a dependence on further "tricks" to get right answers. Consequently, the child's knowledge base is apt to remain at a level inadequate to support higher levels of math.

To improve the quality of teaching and instruction in mathematics for young learners, it should be apparent that a paradigmatic shift is necessary. It also should be clear that for teachers and principals to make this shift, they will need to confront the compelling body of evidence that the best way for children to construct math relationships is in classrooms where thinking and problem solving are valued and encouraged. For those children who lack interest and/or are doing poorly in math, it is even more critical that they engage in active thinking so that their math knowledge base and interest will grow and develop. Educators must provide young children with the best classroom environments possible to encourage thinking. Let us begin by getting rid of the step-by-mindless-step rules to get right answers and let the children think.

* * * * *

An earlier version of this chapter, entitled "Thinking about Math Thinking," was published in the Spring 1997 issue of *Kappa Delta Pi Record,* published by Kappa Delta Pi, an International Honor Society in Education. Used with permission.

CHAPTER 2

SUPPORTING MATH THINKING

"Wrong ideas have to be modified by the child. They can not be taught by the teacher."
— Constance Kamii (1985, p. 36)

Recently a group of us were reminiscing about the games we remembered playing when we were young children. After naming all the familiar games such as War, Go Fish, Concentration, Twenty Questions, Old Maid, Rummy, Parcheesi, I'm Going on a Trip, etc., we started talking about fondly remembered family rituals. One woman reminisced about going with her sister to visit her grandfather. It was their special treat to divide equally between them any pennies he'd collected since their last visit. She remembers the concentration needed to make certain there were no mistakes, and if there were a penny left over, it went back into the penny dish for the next visit. Another women remembered the ritual of Saturday night treats which her dad brought home for his nine children to share. She described how all of them would sit around the dining room table with a paper cup eagerly awaiting the distribution. All was quiet but the "plink, plink, plink" of M&M's dropping into first one cup and then the next. What couldn't be divided evenly was Mom's. In my family, the rule was

that when one sister divided the candy bar, the other sister got first pick. We formed the relationship of "half" and "equal" early at our house.

Just as each child's disposition and ability to read benefits immeasurably from being read nursery rhymes and picture books, so do children acquire a sense of number when they have early opportunities to think about "number in action." Parents who provide opportunities for children to share equally, to make intelligent guesses, and to play simple board and card games, offer their children thinking challenges that develop their number sense. When children come to school without this kind of previous experience, they are handicapped disproportionately by math programs which assume that math relationships can be taught directly by the teacher according to the curriculum rather than constructed by each child according to that child's level of previous knowledge.

Sometimes parents and teachers think that they are teaching children only when they tell them directly how to do something, as with the rote learning of

ABC's and 1-2-3's. However, children learn much more than memorized letters and numbers when they use letters and numbers to accomplish what they themselves want to do. The normal interaction of children at play (e.g., figuring out how many spaces to move according to the roll of the dice, how many cards make fifteen or what the "chance" card requires) provides natural reading and number thinking challenges.

The Role of Active Thinking

Adults have formed their understanding for adding and subtracting the so-called basic math facts, counting, and number correspondence so long ago, that it is hard for them to identify with the internal struggle young children experience as they attempt to form these relationships for themselves. Many of us have experienced the insufficiency of directing a child to count the spaces "peck, peck, peck" around the game board. If he or she has not formed a one-to-one correspondence of number to space, you might as well save your breath. Most of us have noted how very young children count beyond ten. I remember my own daughter saying twelve-teen, (often skipping thirteen, which didn't fit the pattern she'd formed), and then on to fourteen, fifteen, etc. Recently, I heard a four-year-old counting in the hallway outside my office. He counted up to ten, and I perked my ears to listen, as he went on to "tenty-one, tenty-two." No one had ever taught him "tenty-one and tenty-

two" for eleven and twelve, nor had he ever heard it. He invented it himself. It probably was based on what he already knew about twenty-one, twenty-two and thirty-one, thirty-two. When adults look beyond these "errors" made by young children, they often find that children make them because they are thinking and working to make sense of what interests them.

I've heard educators say "problem solving and thinking is fine, but certain things like math facts and multiplication tables must be memorized." Unfortunately, to some teachers and parents that means only one thing: providing the drill and practice of worksheets, flash cards and other rote activities. These people seem to have a "no-pain-no-gain" mentality about learning math facts. The very name "math facts" implies that these "facts" are simply external data to be memorized through practice rather than internal relationships to be constructed by thinking. In workshops on creating supportive math environments, I ask teachers to think back to how they felt as children when asked to do worksheets. Occasionally, someone will say that they *liked* doing worksheets. At first, that shocked me, as I have no such memory for the dreary task. But, I suppose, if you were among the students who could work the answers and got a special bang out of gold stars and teacher praise, you might remember them more fondly. There is a profound dilemma inherent in the drill-and-practice mentality of using worksheets to teach early math relationships. Since children have to *know* these relationships in order to *do* the worksheets, what possible purpose do they serve? If you already know your "math facts", you surely do not need the worksheets. For those who do not know them, the worksheet does nothing to teach them. It simply serves as a reminder to these children of their continual failure in math.

Children *do* benefit by committing to memory what has come to be known as "math facts." However, passively learning them by rote as described above is not only unpleasant, but may also be counterproductive. When "memorizing" prevents children from actively thinking and "figuring out" solutions for themselves, there is very little, if any, mental growth. The children's previous knowledge base will not develop without thinking, and therefore, will not support the ever more complex number challenges to come.

Let us consider what teachers and parents can do to replace the traditional drill-and-practice approach to memorizing "math facts." Children use their natural ability to think when confronted with number problems. When they add two numbers less than ten, they count off the first number then continue their count with the second number to arrive at the total. It is the classic counting-on-your-fingers method of figuring out a problem. (And, as you may guess, it is no coincidence that base-ten number systems prevail throughout the world.) Repetition does contribute to remembering, but the passive, rote practice of worksheets is boring and usually by-passes active thinking. Thinking must accompany repetition so that the double pay-off of constructing the knowledge base *along* with remembering the "math fact" is realized.

Dice, card and board games offer perfect opportunities for children to figure out solutions to adding small numbers together repeatedly. Children will play these games over and over and over and beg for "just one more." In fact, one principal invited me into his office to talk about the math game fever that had "invaded" his elementary school. He couldn't believe that the children preferred playing math games to going out for recess! He had never seen such interest in math in his thirty-plus years in education.

Very young children can match spots on the cards or dots on dice to matching configurations on their game board in bingo-type games. (We call them "cover-up" games.) When game boards with numerals are added, children stretch to meet the new demand of matching spots or dots with number. Remember playing War? It is a perfect card game for beginners as they consider which card's number is higher. They can play this game whether they know the number value or not. If they don't know, they can count the card markings for themselves. The games become more complex as children match, compare or add the cards or dice. For example, Double War with two packs of cards utilizing the small-number cards offer young children many addition problems to solve as they figure out which player has the higher sum. Typically, the children happily play the games time and time again until they no longer have to "figure out" that 6 and 3 are 9 or 5 and 3 are 8; they know it. Repetition with active thinking will also lead to remembering. But, best of all, because it involves the children mentally, it leads to the construction of their number sense as well.

The Role of Social Interaction

Children learn and improve their understanding of number as they encounter new and varied number experiences which challenge their previous understanding. Logical ideas about number are formed gradually, often over long periods of time. Illogical or less efficient ideas are changed as new experiences challenge the child's earlier notions. The debate and exchange of viewpoint which occurs naturally during dice, card and board games encourage children to examine their own thinking. Let me give an example. Two kindergartners, Kim and Terri, were playing a simple board game. A spinner was spun to indicate how many moves to take on the board. Kim continually counted the space of his present location, which he had reached on his last turn, as the first space of his present turn. At first, Terri did not

notice this but eventually saw what was happening. Recognizing that this was not the way counting worked, Terri endeavored to give Kim a "lesson" on how to "count on" from his present location. Her first explanation consisted of directions to "do it like this: one, two, three, four, five." But, Kim could not make the mental connection. There was too big a gap between his level of understanding and what Terri was showing him. As far as he was concerned "one, two, three, four, five" was exactly the way he WAS doing it. Finally, in exasperation, Terri told him "no, do it like this: "um, one, two, three, four, five." Even though Terri did not have the word for zero, she could conceptualize that the space your marker was already on was before "one." She didn't have the word so she created "um." And, Kim went on with his turn starting with "um" for the place where his game marker already was then "one, two, three, four, five" forward on the game board. It is likely that Terri learned more from her own "lesson" by forming it than Kim did by observing it. Kim may or may not be executing Terri's directions by rote without reflection. On the other hand, Terri took on the task of explaining an important concept about counting which was barely within her ability to conceptualize herself. This requires intensely focused thinking. It is precisely this kind of thinking that leads to better understanding which then supports ever more complex mental structures. The question parents and teachers need to be asking is "what kind of learning environment fosters and supports this kind of focused thinking?" Part of the answer to this question should include the opportunity for the exchange of viewpoint bound to occur when children interact.

The Role of Previous Knowledge

Playing dice, card and board games offer continual thinking challenges for the children playing them. Many times the number thinking inherent in game play goes unnoticed by adult observers who focus their attention on the rules and game pieces rather than the thinking they provoke. Often, a child's response is misinterpreted by an adult perspective. I will describe an example. One day I was observing math games in a second-grade classroom. I moved toward one circle of children who were playing Quince, a version of Black Jack with any number instead of only 21. Each day the children checked the chalkboard to see what number the teacher had designated as "quince." It could be any number, 22 or 18 or 13, but today it was 15. A little girl was dealing, and she insisted that I join the group. So I did. She was quite concerned that I have a successful experience and took great pains to explain that I must not go over 15. She dealt a card to each of us, then asked us, did we want another "hit." Her previous card-playing experience was readily apparent as she handled the deck. She

paused again to make sure I understood that I could not go over 15 and asked me if I wanted another card. I had such a low card I was in no danger. My "hit" was another low card. The game slowed down as children struggled to make their calculations. They were adding cards together, subtracting from 15 and confronting the probability of the next card. All of these mathematical operations were stretching their mental limits. There was no talking as each player was consumed with his or her task. All but me. I had two cards that added up to five and was unconcerned about a third "hit." By my fourth "hit," the dealer was getting very nervous for me, and inquired again to make sure I understood the rule. As beginner's luck would have it, my fifth card gave me exactly 15! Immediately, I called "quince" and laid down my five cards as evidence. The little boy to my right snapped his head around to look and said "How'd she do that?" My adult interpretation of his question was that he, along with me, couldn't believe the unlikely probability of having only 15 points with so many cards. Later I realized that wasn't what he meant at all. He could not fathom and was marveling at another most unlikely probability. As he was still struggling with his calculations, it was beyond his comprehension to imagine that anyone could add together five cards so quickly. Here were two totally different interpretations based on two very different levels of experience with number calculations.

Piaget said that children cannot see, hear or remember that which they cannot understand. If the mental structures are not in place to support what is seen or heard, there will be no mental connection and consequently it will not be recognized or remembered. I am reminded of this phenomenon each time I hear a new word that I am sure I have never heard before. Later I am amazed when I hear that same word three times the following week. Had I never heard the word before or had I never mentally connected to what had no meaning for me? The previous knowledge level of the learner plays a critical role as the learner struggles to figure out how to reconcile new information with the old. If the gap is too great between what is understood and the new information, there will be no mental "wrestling" and, consequently, no new understanding constructed. Every teacher is aware of what can occur when there is not *enough* challenge to previous knowledge and interest is lost and attention drifts. If new learning does not "hook" into the understanding for what has been learned previously, it will not last. That is one of the reasons that the spelling words memorized for last Friday's test are misspelled on Monday's creative writing project. It most likely why "cramming" for an exam rarely results in lasting knowledge. We teachers must continually be mindful of the previous knowledge base of all our students.

The Role of Choice

Child-initiated choice plays another important role in learning. When children have real opportunities to choose to do something (e.g., which book to read, what to build or pretend, which toy or game to play), it is because they want to. When choice is freely made, it is driven by interest. And, interest offers distinct opportunities to practice the important dispositions of initiative and curiosity. Children with initiative and curiosity are in a good position to develop other positive dispositions such as persistence and industry. As all teachers well know, developing or not developing these dispositions will profoundly affect the child for rest of his or her life.

Interest is, of course, very much related to what the child already knows. Children tend to be interested in something that varies "moderately" from what they already understand. A new twist on a familiar game often will captivate a child's attention. For the most part, teachers are very good at determining what is "age appropriate" for the children in their classes. However, it is more difficult to understand the fine tuning of what makes something "individually appropriate." Constructivist teachers know that to understand what is individually appropriate for young children, they must observe the children as they make choices for themselves.

A second-grade teacher told me about Sallie, a little girl in her class who was very weak in math. The only math game Sallie would play was a version of Go Fish. Instead of matching pairs of cards as in the original version, the objective of this game was to make pairs that add to ten. Sallie had played the game with everyone in the class several times and was having a hard time trying to find someone who would play it yet again. The game was no longer "moderately novel" to her classmates. They had moved on to more challenging games. The consequence of letting children choose their own games and partners in this case had created a problem for Sallie to resolve. If she wanted to play, she would have to learn a new game. Her desire to play was stronger than her reluctance to try something new. An alert teacher helped her along by introducing her to a "moderately novel" game. That was all she needed, and she was ready for another round of play. Slowly, Sallie's repertory of games increased. She never was a math whiz but she enjoyed some of the math games and, consequently, continued to build her mathematical knowledge base in second grade.

Sallie continued to choose the same game over and over for a very good reason. Children usually do not choose to do what they are unable to do. Sallie was still getting as much challenge from repeating Go Fish as she could handle. If the teacher had assigned game partners and games or produced a work sheet, Sallie might have experienced even less success than she did. When children have trouble working math problems assigned to them, they tend to focus on their failure and mistakes rather than on what they are doing correctly. When this scenario is repeated enough, children come to see themselves as being "dumb" in math.

One of the happy consequences of letting children choose is that children rarely choose to do what they are incapable of doing. Consequently, choice almost always ensures success. When children are successful, they feel confident about what they can do. They see themselves as being "smart." Self esteem develops when children see themselves as competent. This sense of success and competence leads to the creation of an optimal environment for further learning.

Thus, a constructive, positive cycle is likely to occur when teachers allow for child-initiated choice in their classrooms. Choice reflects the child's interest and is likely to represent moderate difficulty. Choice ensures success which leads to increased confidence that comes from feeling competent. This, in turn, creates a classroom climate which is ideal for making more challenging choices which leads to further interest, success, confidence and even greater competence. Consequently, teachers who provide opportunities for choice in the classroom ensure that their students have "individually appropriate" challenges available to them throughout the school day.

The Role of Mistakes

It has always baffled me that some teachers work so hard to promote self-esteem in children yet simultaneously give children inappropriate academic tasks to perform. Some teachers fail to recognize how a child's response is *on the way to being right*. Children develop self-confidence from experiencing success. Teachers' praise, sticker awards and "All About Me" theme projects will not alter the perception children have of themselves if failure to succeed dominates their day.

I am reminded of a kindergarten boy who would not show me the sentence he had just written on the computer because not all the words were spelled correctly. I was delighted that he had phonemic awareness and could work independently at the computer. However, even though he was obviously very advanced, instead of being pleased with his accomplishment, he was anxious about his lack of perfection and felt inadequate. His writing brought him far less satisfaction than another child who busily and thoughtfully wrote sentence after sentence in his journal using a less advanced level of invented spelling. All other characteristics of these two five-year-olds being equal, who is more likely to develop the disposition to be a writer? Recognizing what is "right" about a young child's work or response in math requires teachers to have a more complete understanding for logico-mathematical thinking. For example, when children

count to ten, what do they actually know about those numbers? Can they count ten items with one-to-one correspondence of one number to one item? When the teacher says, "show me eight chips," do they point to the eighth chip or to a collection of eight chips? When children add two collections together, can they "count on" from the first collection (e.g., 4 + 3 = "4, 5, 6, 7") or must they start from "one" (i.e., "1, 2, 3, 4, 5, 6, 7")? Which dice do the children choose to use, the dice with dots or numerals? What happens when they have one of each? Little Becky proudly showed me three fingers to her daddy's request to tell me how old she was. "Becky's this many," I replied smiling and holding up one finger on one hand and two on the other. "Oh, no," Becky responded and showed me again her one-handed version of three fingers. All day long, teachers observe young children as they reveal their incomplete understanding for their world.

What purpose does it serve to point out that the child's level of understanding is wrong according to our adult standard? Can Becky's daddy show Becky all the different ways to represent three with her fingers? Of course, the real issue here is *should* he do this or will Becky figure it out for herself in time? Could teaching Becky directly, negatively affect her disposition to figure things out for herself? Does it unnaturally emphasize to her what she does wrong rather than accept what is *on the way to being right?* What teachers and parents alike *should* be doing is providing environments that encourage children to think and figure things out for themselves. What kind of environment will support both the perfectionist kindergartner and the experienced-impoverished child to read, write and compute? Certainly, a part of the answer lies in the acceptance of developmental errors as *on the way to being right*.

The Role of Self-Direction

In a conversation about encouraging self-motivation and control in young children, one kindergarten teacher told of Leslie, a little girl in her class who was at the easel, paint brush in hand and ready to paint. She asked her teacher what she should paint. Her teacher said to paint something that *she*, Leslie, *wanted* to paint. To this, Leslie replied that she wanted to paint what the teacher wanted her to paint.

This child's experience with life, as limited as it had been in five short years, taught her a role that society especially values in women: that of consideration and concern for others. And what could possibly be wrong with that? Consideration and concern for others is certainly a goal we have for all young children. However, when it is so extreme that it is more like subservience, it can be detrimental. When children, girls or boys, blindly conform to the teachers wishes, they are missing an important opportunity to think for themselves. Since thinking builds upon thinking, when children think *less*, a sequence of events begins that could ultimately lead to learning less, or more precisely, to constructing less intellectual power. Let us imagine what happens to this little girl (and to many others like her) when her need to please her teacher is combined with math instruction. If the teacher teaches children to add and subtract by using conventional algorithms, the blind conformity could continue. For example, do you remember how you were taught to do double-digit addition? You learned, probably, to execute a series of steps which, if you were meticulous in your execution, would lead you to the correct answer. Although the National Council of Teachers of Mathematics and others are calling for more problem solving in the primary classroom, most children are still learning to do math problems by memorizing steps. The unfortunate consequence of this method of teaching mathematical operations is that children do not need to think about the essence of the problem to solve it. They merely go from step one to step two, etc. until they reach the answer and a nod of approval (or disapproval) from their teacher. Since thinking is necessary to construct knowledge, children who reach correct solutions without thoughtful engagement may please their teacher but they will not construct their number sense. Children who do not construct a sense of number will not have a sufficient knowledge base to support more complex math operations where thinking is a requirement such as in algebra and geometry.

There is a social dimension to self-direction in the classroom that must be addressed. Just as children benefit intellectually from being self-directed, there are some social advantages as well. If children are given choices in the classroom and allowed to interact with other children, they need to be self-disciplined, as well as self-directed. If control of your students is a big issue with you or your principal, it will be difficult to nearly impossible to create the supportive environment described in this chapter. Believe me, children will be out of their seats and talking. If they are thinking, they may challenge, albeit politely, *your* thinking. They have been known to ask for proof. I know of a substitute teacher who was "undone" by Freda, a second grader who called out "I disagree" to another student's math solution. The autonomous class indignantly reported the substitute teacher's controlling reactions in this incident to their regular teacher the next morning. Changing from teacher control to student self-control cannot be accomplished overnight. Somewhat ironically, however, children in this kind of constructive environment are more likely to construct self-direction and control than children who are not. Which of our little girls will be more likely to say "No" to pressure from her teenage peers? Will it be the one who

blindly conforms to her teacher's direction or the one who calls out, "I disagree" when she see a better way? Just as children who think construct their intellect and competence, so do children who use self-control learn to become more self-controlled and confident in their socio-moral choices. So, how do you get on this merry-go-round (or is it off)?

Begin with a familiar game that can be adapted to support your math objectives. For example, Double War can be used to practice addition, subtraction or multiplication. Take out the face cards and the numbers you are not using yet from two decks, and begin. Let the children "invent" their own score keeping or tell them a way you saw other children keeping score that they could try using. The idea is to have the children assume responsibility for as much of the activity as they are capable of doing. Older children can even make their own number cards on the computer then color the spots. You can laminate them so they will last longer. In addition to the satisfaction, there are some other advantages to making your own cards. You can eliminate the "extra" spot under the number on the corners. These spots invariably confuse the youngest children who meticulously count them along with the ones representing the number. Also, we replace the Ace with 1, add 0, and drop the Jack, Queen, and King. Some parents feel that playing cards have no place in school, so we call our creation "counting" cards instead.

You may also begin by asking the children to suggest solutions to a real problem in the class. One first-grade teacher told me that their math time at the end of the school day was always being interrupted with fire drills, school announcements and assemblies. The children were upset about this because they really enjoyed their math time. (You may be skeptical, but I hear this quite a lot.) They had a class meeting and voted to exchange math time with an earlier recess slot. When children solve their own problems and are accountable for the consequences, they become more confident in their ability as problem solvers. As your students become more self-directed and self-controlled, your classroom will become a more supportive environment for thinking and learning. Let the games begin!

* * * * *

A version of this chapter is scheduled to appear in a future issue of PHI DELTA KAPPAN.

CHAPTER 3

LET THE GAMES BEGIN!

"Games lubricate the body and the mind. " - Benjamin Franklin

Reinventing math instruction can begin for you by trying a few games with your students. If your students are inexperienced with game play, you might want to include yourself in the game. For example, I know a pre-school teacher who starts a game of Pick-up Five by sitting on the floor with one child. First, the teacher removes all cards five and higher from a deck of giant playing cards. Next, she places six cards, face-up, in a row. The object is for the child to pick up all pairs that add to five. Inevitably, another eager child or two will come along to take a turn. As the cards are picked up, the teacher replaces them with other cards from the deck for the next player. The teacher can remain in the role of dealer for as long as she feels her presence is necessary. Usually it is not long before a student will take over that role allowing the teacher to introduce another game elsewhere in the room.

This same teacher does a missing addend game that I would never have guessed pre-schoolers would be able to do. She puts some chips in one hand and asks the players to count how many chips she has. Next she drops a few of the chips into her other hand which she keeps closed. She shows the players how many of the chips still remain in the original hand and then asks them to think how many chips are in the closed hand. At the beginning of the school year, she started with three or four chips. By February she was up to eight.

I shared these two games with two special needs teachers. They wanted to try games with their emotionally disturbed and autistic students, but they felt they needed to be directly involved in their children's play. The teachers felt that the social interaction required of most games would be too much for these particular groups of children. Although the teacher can surely play any of the games with their students, the goal should remain that the students always do for themselves what they are capable of doing.

BINGO was my first experience with a cover-up game. It has most of the necessary components of a cover-up game: a game board and a means of generating numbers for the players to match with the numbers on their game board. However, is it age- and individually appropriate for our target population? What kind of mathematical thinking does it require? Identifying double-digit numbers in the columns represented with the letters in B-I-N-G-O may make it too difficult for younger children. Simply matching the spoken numeral to the written numeral is too easy for older children. Offering math games to children which are both appropriate and engaging will require some careful thinking, selection, and perhaps some re-design and invention on the part of the teacher.

Depending on the previous experience of the children, different games offer multiple ways to engage in mathematical thinking. If your students have little number experience, a good beginning game is DOMINO COVER-UP which is included in this chapter. When it is played with one die with dots arranged in the same pattern as the dots on the dominoes, it is a simple matching game involving turn-taking. It can be made more complex by playing it with two dice and matching the roll of the dice with both ends of the domino. Or, for a different mental stretch, let the

children choose dice with numerals instead of dots.

Seven Snakes is a favorite early game, a version of which I first saw described in <u>Mailbox Magazine</u>. Children roll two dice and add the dots to determine which number to cover on their game board. If they roll a seven, they must take a snake. (We used those wiggly fishing worms.) The first person to cover his or her game board *without* accumulating seven snakes is the winner. In the version I've seen children play most often, the winner is determined by who gets seven snakes first! This is a perfect game for first graders just learning to add. Doesn't this sound like more fun than a work sheet of addends through six? If the player doesn't know that five and three is eight, he or she can count the dots to figure it out. More advanced children may think, I know that five and one is six and two more is eight. Eventually, by repeatedly thinking to figure out the answer, the children remember that three and five is eight, without counting or piggy backing on another known relationship. A similar game included in this chapter is SIX WHISKERS COVER-UP. It is played the same way as Seven Snakes, but the children collect whiskers for a leopard every time they roll a six.

There are challenging cover-up games for older children as well. For example, MONSTER MOUTH MATH COVER-UP requires children to think of what two numbers added together are equal to a number on their game board.

Do you remember how you learned to do missing addends? Further challenge is created when children must think of what two numbers MULTIPLIED together are equal a number on their game board.

SINK IT and LEAP FROG COVER-UP require players to form more complex solutions by deciding which math operation is necessary to obtain a particular number on their game board. By using three dice, the players have even more possibilities to consider.

Before you try these games with your students, I want to emphasize once again the important role that free-choice plays in the construction of math logic. By allowing children to choose which game they play, the teacher increases the probability that each child is more interested, acts more responsibly and is mentally engaged. This offers the best possible opportunity for each child to build upon his or her previous knowledge base no matter how divergent that base is from the grade "norm." Every teacher is well aware of the wide range of levels that children have in the same grade. When children may choose from a variety of games, the teacher is appropriately individualizing math instruction. The children are much more likely to learn in an environment where choice prevails.

Start by carefully tearing out a game and coloring it. Next, assemble as necessary. We trimmed the four-piece game boards, leaving a border on two of the parts diagonal to one another. These borders then supported the other two trimmed diagonal pieces and were easily pasted together. Positioning the game boards, chance cards and counting cards on poster board and then laminating them increased the life of the games. Some teachers found that attaching the laminated, one-piece game boards (e.g., SIX WHISKERS COVER) together with a brass fastener in the upper right-hand corner, then "fanning" them open for play, helped younger children with turn-taking. The next step is to watch the children play and think!

DOMINO COVER-UP

Good Game for: Number recognition, matching dots or numerals

Of Interest for Ages: 5-7 years   **Number of Players:** 2

Materials Needed to Play: Standard domino set with zero to six dots per side
or domino cards, 2 dice, cover-up chips (2 colors)

Make Your Own Materials: Remove carefully and laminate the Domino Coverup cards
to extend their life. We used the see-through plastic BINGO chips for coverup chips.

Set-up to Play: All dominoes are placed face-side up between the two players. Each
player uses a different color of cover-up chips. See illustration on page 16.

Game Rules:
1. Players roll one die to determine play. High roll goes first.
2. First player rolls the two dice then looks for the domino that matches that roll.
   For example, if a 5 and a 6 are rolled, the player must find the domino with
   five dots on one end and six dots on the other. After the first player finds the
   domino that matches his or her roll, he or she claims the domino by covering
   each end with his or her colored chip. The turn then passes to the other
   player. If there is no domino to match the roll, there is no play and the turn
   passes to the other player.
3. Play continues until all the dominoes have been claimed.
4. The player who claims the most dominoes is the winner.

Object of the Game: To make more matches and claim more dominoes.

Game Variations: This game can be played with numerals instead of dots on the dice
or a combination of dots and numerals on the dice. Very young children can play
with one die. When they find a match with one end of a domino, they cover only
that end of the domino with a chip. A more strategic game can be played by
older children if they can place their chip on any domino end that matches their
dice roll. This will allow a player to block another player's claim to a domino.

Game History: Adapted from an original game by Jean Carlton, lead teacher in the
infant room at Old Dominion University Child Development Center in Norfolk, VA.

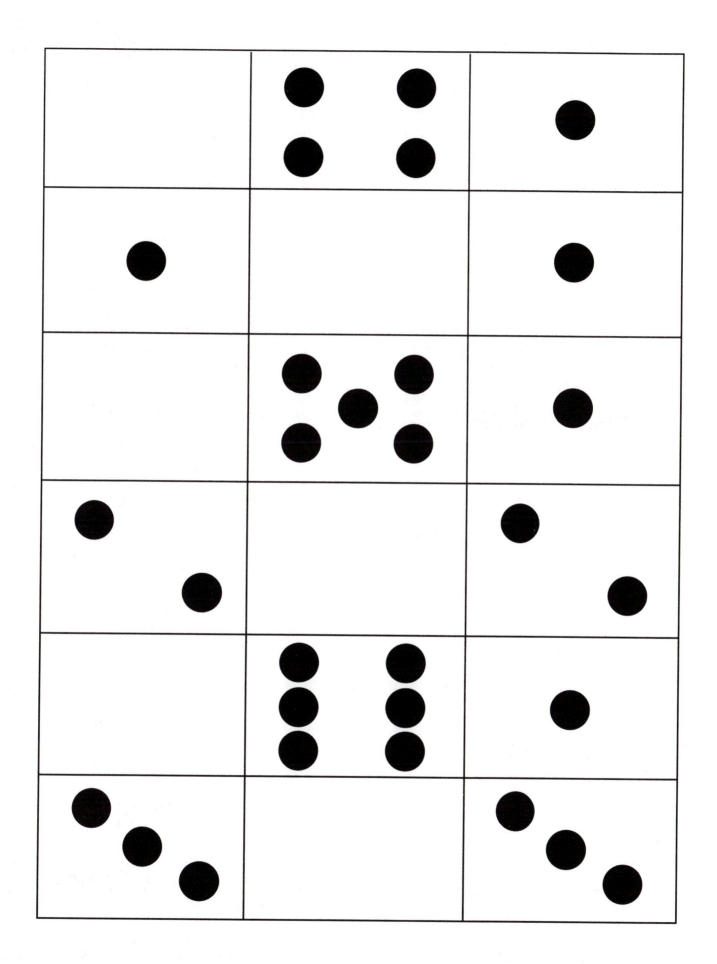

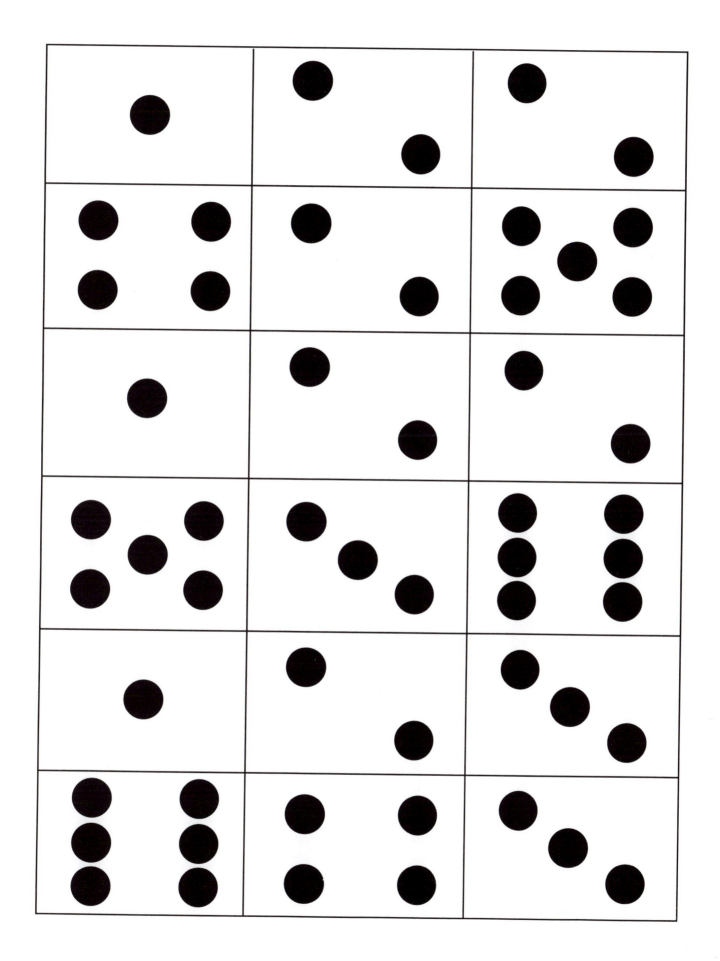

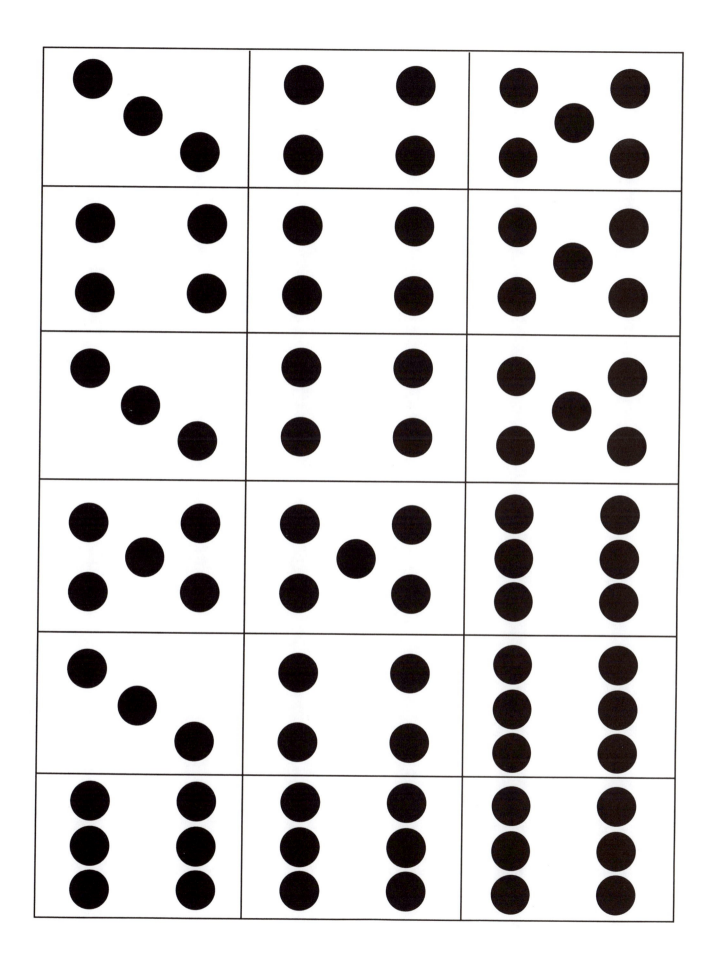

PHONE NUMBER COVER-UP

Good Game for: Addition with addends of 0 to 5, subtraction with numbers 1 to 6

Of Interest for Ages: 5-7 years   **Number of Players:** 2-4

Materials Needed to Play: Laminated sentence strips, erasable marking pens, cover-up chips, 2 dice with dots or numerals

Make Your Own Materials: Laminate some sentence strips. Cut each strip long enough for a seven or ten-digit phone number to be written on it. The children's favorite cover-up chips were the dried lima beans we had spray-painted gold to use for pirate treasure. One teacher provided clip clothespins which were clipped over the number to "cover-up."

Set-up to Play: To begin the game, each player takes a laminated sentence strip and writes his or her phone number on it with an erasable marker. Each player will need seven (or 10) cover-up chips (or clips). See illustration on page 5.

Game Rules:
   1. Use dice to determine who goes first. Play rotates clockwise from player to player around the group.
   2. The player rolls the dice. If the sum or difference of the roll is in the player's phone number, he or she covers that number with a chip.
   3. Play continues until one player has covered up all of the numbers in his or her phone number.

Object of the Game: To be the first player to cover all the numbers in his or her phone number.

Game Variations: Younger children may only want to play using the sum of their roll. For an addition-only game, regular dice must be altered so that a zero and one can be rolled. This is easily accomplished by placing a sticky dot over each six and labeling it with a zero. To vary the phone numbers, the children enjoyed looking in the phone directory for numbers of their favorite fast-food restaurants or stores.

Game History: Adapted from an original game by Sharon McGlohn, 1st-grade teacher at Abingdon Elementary School in Gloucester, VA.

SIX WHISKERS COVER-UP

Good Game for: Addition with addends 1 to 6, emphasizing totals of 6

Of Interest for Ages: 5-7 years   **Number of Players:** 2-4

Materials Needed to Play: Laminated leopard game boards, cover-up "spots," pipe-cleaner whiskers, 2 dice with dots or numerals

Make Your Own Materials: Color and laminate leopard game boards. Cut one-inch circles from black construction paper to make "spots," then laminate them. To make the whiskers, cut black pipe cleaners into one-and-one-half inch lengths.

Set-up to Play: To begin the game, each player takes a leopard game board, 10 "spots," and 6 whiskers.

Game Rules:
1. Use dice to determine who goes first. Play rotates clockwise from player to player around the group.
2. The first player rolls the dice and covers up the sum of his or her roll.
3. Since there is no number 6 on the leopard game board to cover up, anytime a 6 is rolled, that player must place a whisker on his or her game board. If any player accumulates six whiskers, that player is out of the game and the game continues with the remaining players.
4. Play continues until one player has covered up all of the numbers on his or her leopard game board without accumulating all six whiskers.

Object of the Game: To be the first player to cover up all the numbers on his or her leopard game board before accumulating six whiskers.

Game Variations: Younger children consistently play this game by ignoring rule number three. They are not as likely to be motivated by competition, as older children are. Often they will take turns "winning." They think that if you are "getting" something, such as the whiskers, then you must be "winning." You may want to let the children figure out how to determine the winner of this game for themselves.

Game History: Adapted from an original game by Alicia Milks, teacher-in-training at Old Dominion University in Norfolk, VA.

TIME COVER-UP

Good Game for: Reading time on an analog clock, connecting events with a particular time, matching analog time with digital time

Of Interest for Ages: 6-7 years   **Number of Players:** 2-4

Materials Needed to Play: Clock face game boards, cover-up time cards

Make Your Own Materials: Draw hands on the game board clocks for times that are meaningful to the children playing the game. For example, we used "time for snack, recess, math, lunch, music, library, etc. Each game board of clocks should have some different times (like BINGO cards do). Next, photocopy each game board of clocks to make a second set of clock faces to use as cover-up time cards. Color the clocks if desired, then laminate both the clock game boards and the photocopies. Cut apart each clock face of the photocopies *only* and use as cover-up time cards.

Set-up to Play: To begin the game, each player takes a laminated clock game board. The time cards are shuffled and placed face down in a draw pile convenient to all.

Game Rules:
1. Draw a time card to determine who plays first.
2. The player draws a time card or picks up the discarded time card and looks for a match on his or her clock game board. If a match is found the time card is turned over on top of the clock with the matching time. If there is no match, the drawn card is discarded and play rotates to the next player.
3. Play continues until one player has covered up all of his or her clocks.

Object of the Game: To be the first player to cover-up all of his or her clocks.

Game Variations: Other meaningful times that could be used on the cards could be derived from picture books with time references such as Eric Carle's <u>Grouchy Lady Bug</u>, or <u>Tuesday</u> by David Wiesner. You could try a favorite tv show. Let them help think of the times. For a different challenge, try matching analog clock game boards with cards in which the time is written digitally (e.g., 10:15, 12:00, 2:15)

Game History: Adapted from an original game by Linda Reams, 1st-grade teacher at Petsworth Elementary School in Gloucester, VA.

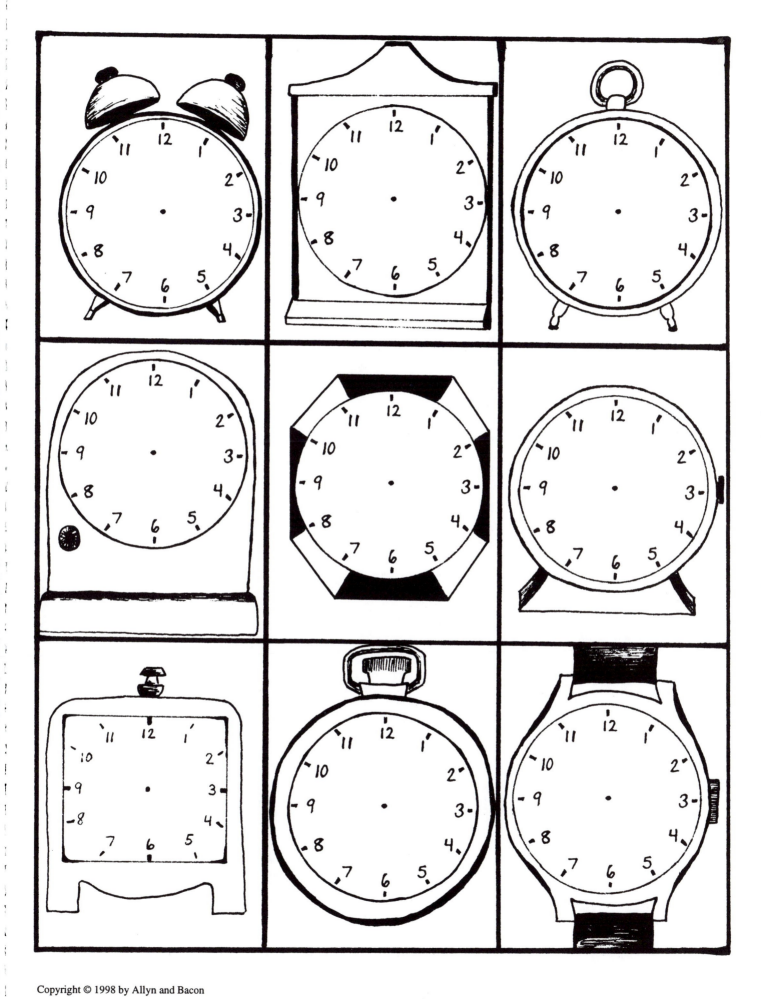

MONSTER MOUTH MATH COVER-UP

Good Game for: Addition with addends 0 to 10, finding the missing addend (multiplication)

Of Interest for Ages: 6-9 years   **Number of Players:** 2-4

Materials Needed to Play: Monster Mouth game boards, erasable marking pens, cover-up chips, 2 decks of counting cards or playing cards

Make Your Own Materials: Photocopy a second deck of 44 counting cards, laminate the two decks and cut cards apart. Laminate the Monster Mouth game boards. We used the dried lima-bean-teeth with "bloody roots" that the children had made for another game as our cover-up chips.

Set-up to Play: Each player takes a laminated Monster Mouth and writes his or her choice of numbers from 0-20 (without duplicating) on the 15 teeth. Each player takes 15 cover-up chips. Five cards are dealt to each player. The remaining cards are placed face down in a draw pile convenient to all players.

Game Rules:
1. Players draw cards to determine who goes first.
2. Play begins as first player draws two cards from the deck. If the sum of these cards and/or any cards in the player's hand is on his or her game board, he or she may cover up that number. The paired cards are removed from play, and play rotates clockwise to the next player.
4. Play continues until one player has covered up all of his or her numbers.

Object of the Game: To be the first player to cover up all of his or her numbers.

Game Variations: Older children enjoy a version of this game using multiplication to play. Before the children write numerals on their monster mouth teeth, one player draws a card which determines the multiplier for the entire game. Knowing the multiplier, the children write products on their teeth. Players proceed to draw a card in turn, multiplying that card with the multiplier and covering up any matching products. We introduced this game at Halloween but it was a favorite all year.

Game History: Adapted from an original game by Maribeth Horner, speech/language pathologist at Cooper Elementary School in Hampton, VA.

MONSTER MATH

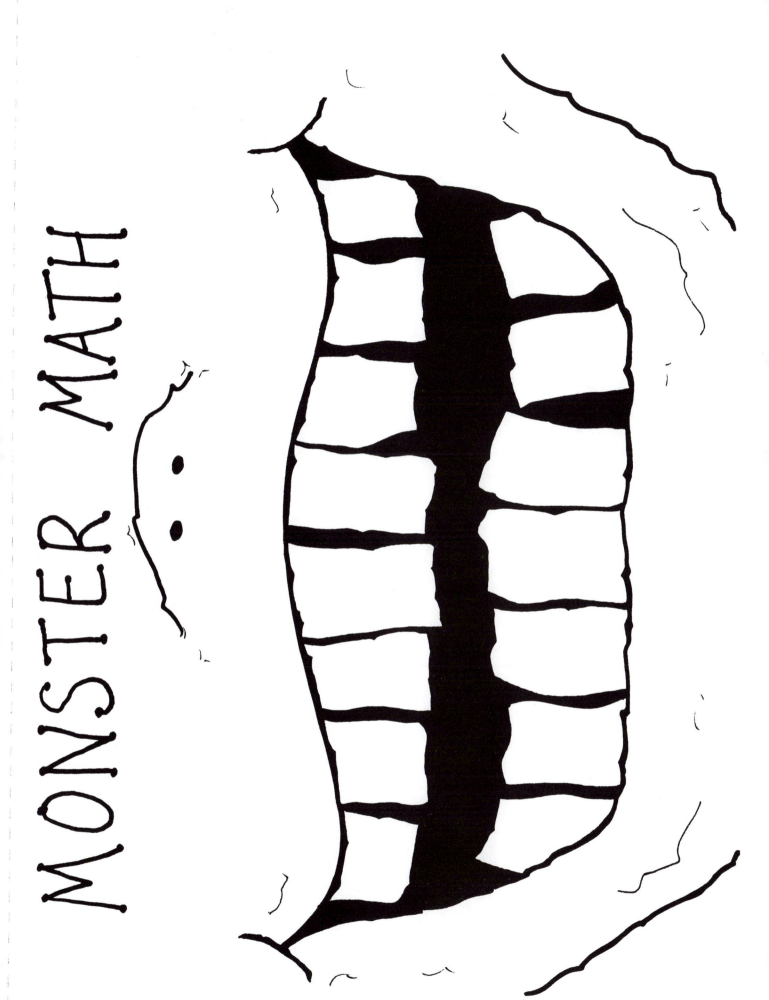

MONSTER MATH

MONSTER MATH

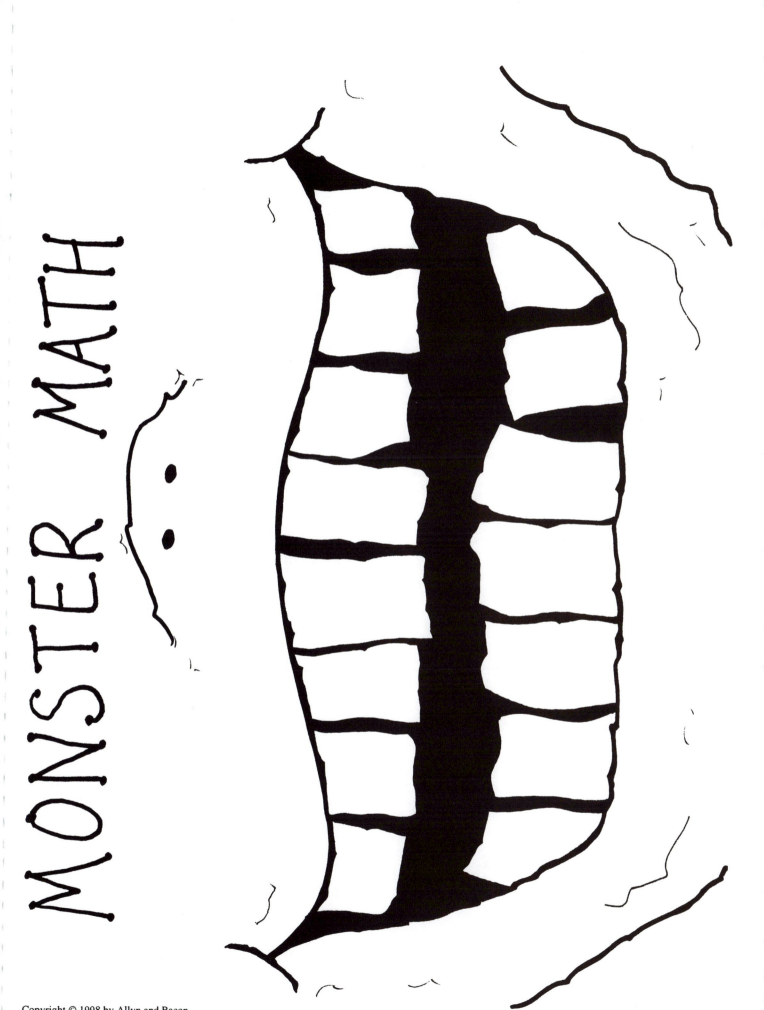

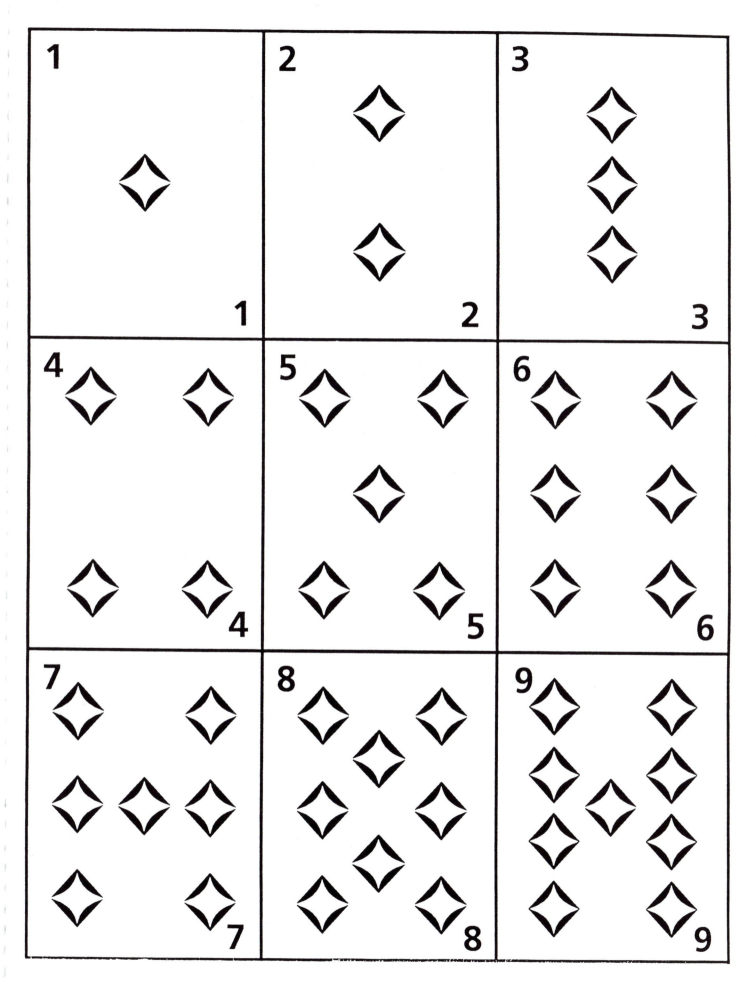

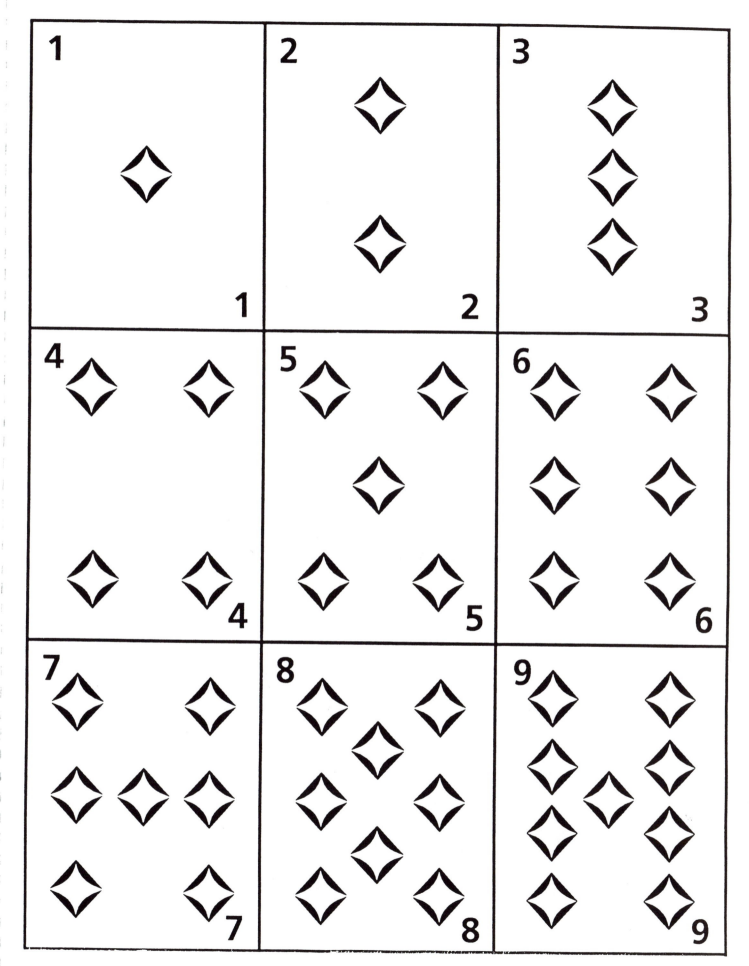

10 ◆ ◆ ◆ ◆ ◆ ◆ ◆ ◆ ◆ ◆ ◆ **10**	**10** ◆ ◆ ◆ ◆ ◆ ◆ ◆ ◆ ◆ ◆ ◆ **10**	**0** **0**
10 ◆ ◆ ◆ ◆ ◆ ◆ ◆ ◆ ◆ ◆ **10**	*COUNTING CARDS* *FOR* *NUMBER GAMES* *(4 each 0 to 10)*	**0** **0**
10 ◆ ◆ ◆ ◆ ◆ ◆ ◆ ◆ ◆ ◆ ◆ **10**	**0** **0**	**0** **0**

LEAP FROG COVER-UP

Good Game for: Addition, subtraction, multiplication, division, 2-step problems

Of Interest for Ages: 8-10 years   **Number of Players:** 2-4

Materials Needed to Play: Individual game board ladders, cover-up chips, 2-3 dice

Make Your Own Materials: Color and laminate the Leap Frog game board ladders. Using an erasable marker, add numbers according to the ability of the players.

Set-up to Play: Each player takes a game board ladder and 7 cover-up chips.

Game Rules:
1. Use dice to determine order of play. Play rotates clockwise from player to player.
2. The player rolls 2-3 dice and tries to form an equation from the roll to equal the number on any one of the spaces of the next rung of his or her game board ladder. Any of the four math operations may be used with the numbers of the dice roll. (E.g., If the player needs a 33 and the dice roll is a 3, 5 and 6, the player can multiply 5x6=30 then add 3 to reach 33.) If the player can form an equation that equals a needed number, he or she covers the number with a cover-up chip. If the player cannot form an equation, play rotates to the next player.
3. Play continues until one player covers up one of the three numbers on each of the rungs of his or her game board ladder and reaches the lily pad to win the game.

Object of the Game: To travel up the game board ladder and reach the lily pad before the other players.

Game Variations: This is an excellent game to play with teams. If your students have not had previous experience with games and other mental math activities (as opposed to paper and pencil math), they may find it difficult to follow a series of operations in their heads. If this is a problem, you might want to try team play. Team play was a good bridge to mental math, as the teacher wrote the equations down on the overhead transparency as one student explained how the solution was derived.

Game History: Inspired by Fred Gwynne's story, <u>Pondlarker</u> and adapted from an original game by Chris Brewer, 4th-grade teacher at Portlock Elementary School in Chesapeake, VA.

SINK IT!

Good Game for: Addition, subtraction, multiplication, division, 2-step problems

Of Interest for Ages: 8-10 years   **Number of Players:** 2-4

Materials Needed to Play: Individual submarine game boards, 3 dice, cover-up chips, erasable marking pens

Make Your Own Materials: Color and laminate the submarine game boards. Add numbers to portholes with an erasable marker. The same numbers should be written in the "bubbles" across the top of each game board. Orient the numbers in the "bubbles" so that the other players can read them. The transparent bingo markers make excellent cover-up chips, since players can still see the numbers through them.

Set-up to Play: Each player takes a submarine game board, writes numbers on the portholes and "bubbles" then covers up all the "holes" with chips.

Game Rules:
1. Use dice to determine order of play. Play rotates clockwise from player to player.
2. Each player rolls 3 dice and tries to form an equation from the roll which is equal to a number on any of the covered "holes" of a rival player's submarine OR any of the player's own submarine "holes" that have been "hit" by an opposing player. Any math operation may be used with the three numbers rolled. (E.g., If the player needs 33 and the dice roll is a 3, 5 and 6, the player can add $5+6=11$ then multiply the 11 by 3 to reach 33.) If all numbers can be used, the player uncovers (or covers) that number. If the player cannot, play rotates to the next player.
3. Play continues until all but one submarine have been sunk.

Object of the Game: To uncover the numbers of the opposing player's submarine and to cover any numbers on your own submarine and to be the last submarine afloat.

Game Variations: This game can be made simpler by using only two dice and numbers that can be made with them. This is another good game for team play. Use the overhead projector so that everyone can see the numbers on both submarines.

Game History: Adapted from an original game by Judy Morgan, 3rd-grade teacher at Watkins Elementary School in Newport News, VA.

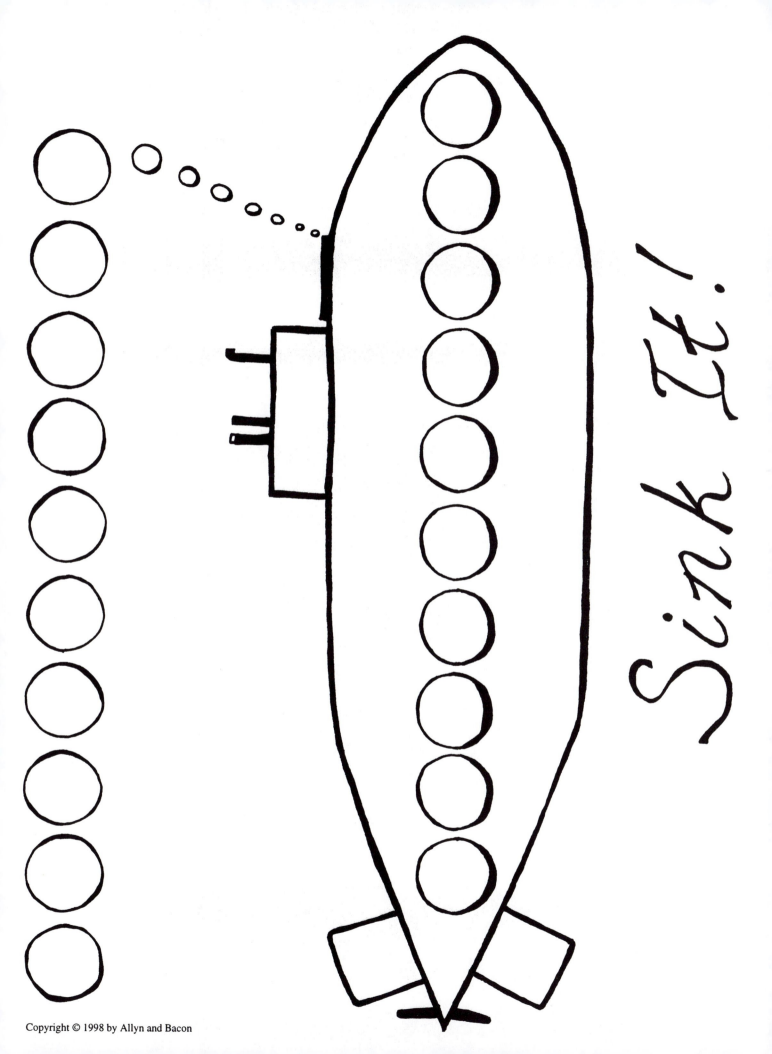

Sink It!

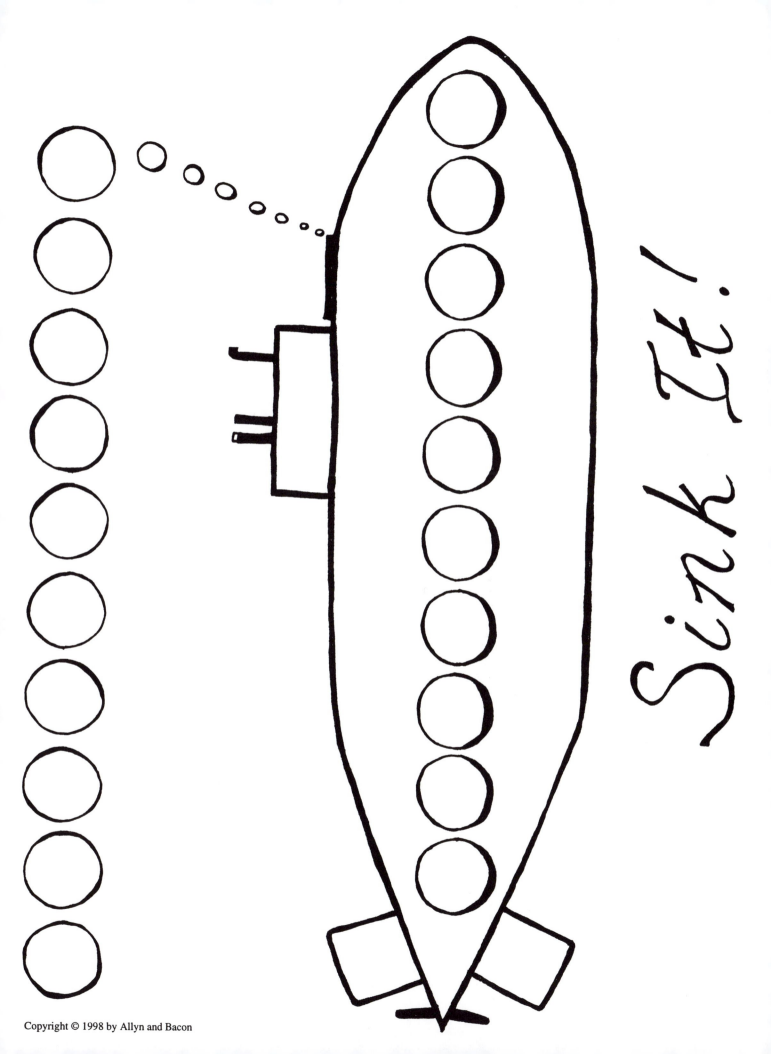

Sink It!

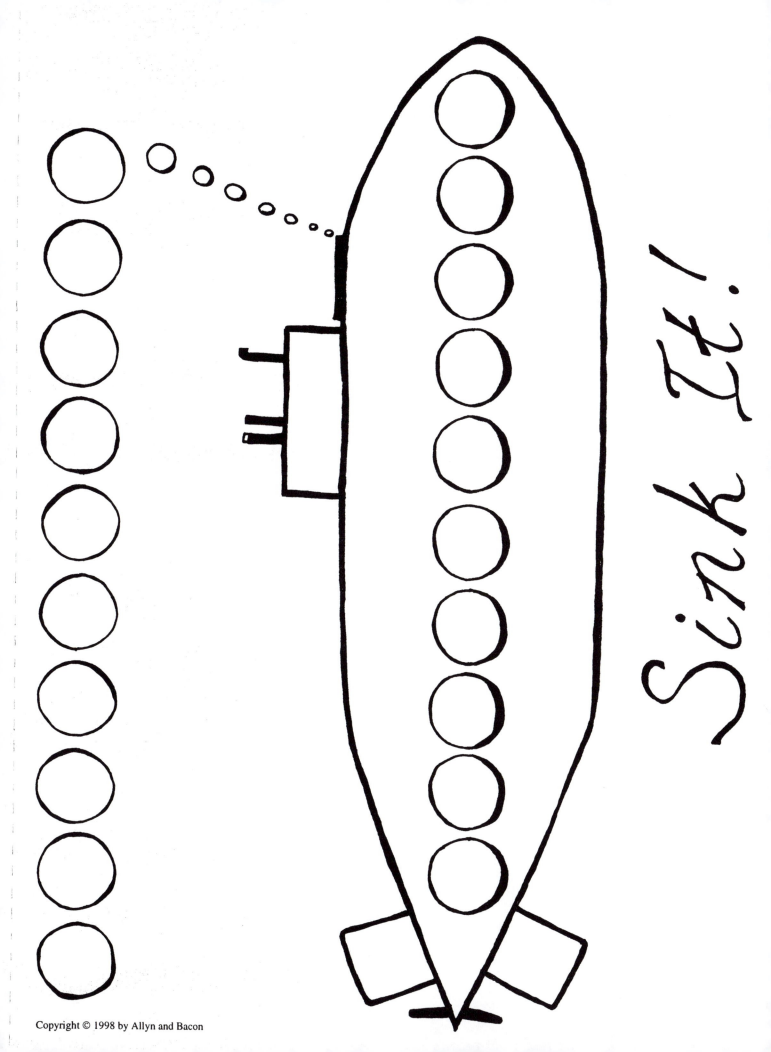

Sink It!

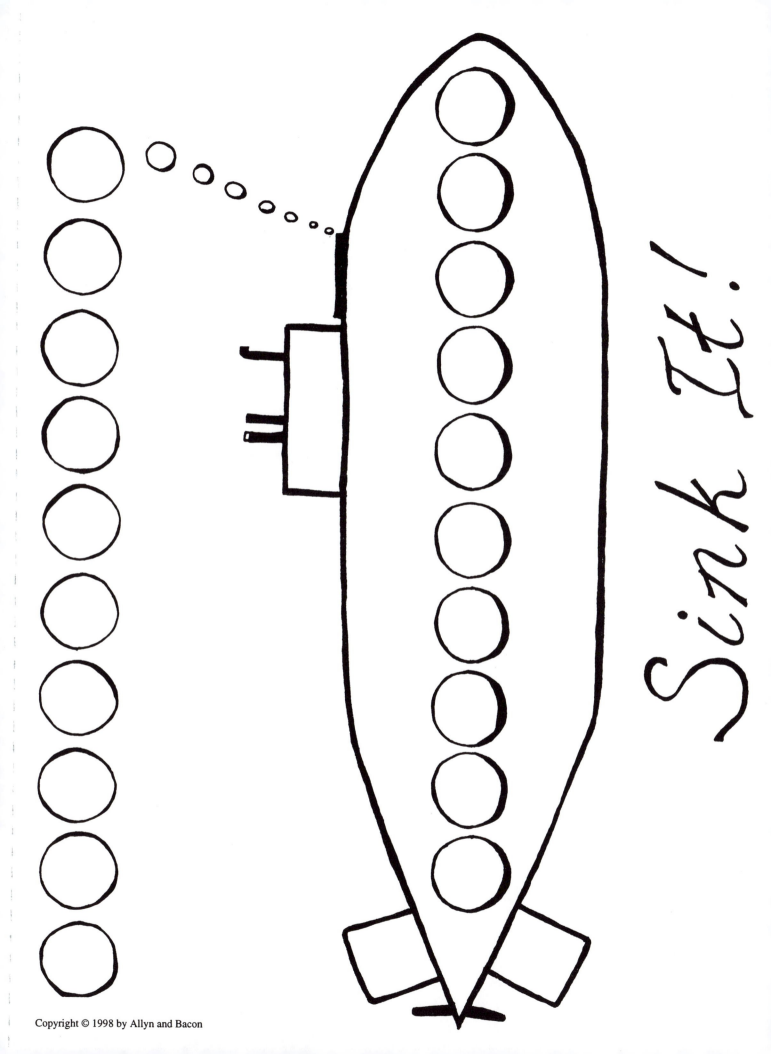

Sink It!

CHAPTER 4

THINKING ABOUT MONEY

"I am always ready to learn, but I do not always like to be taught."
- Winston Churchill

In Chapter Two, I gave examples of how children are able to "count on" from one number to another and from one turn to the next. I picture the construction of this idea about computation as a continuum of evidence representing ever more sophisticated, efficient and complex mental adaptation. On one end of this continuum, the child is quite satisfied to "count all" when adding two numbers. Many children will use their fingers as they count. Teachers recognize one case of "counting all," as in the problem of 4+3, when the child counts off the first number: 1, 2, 3, *four* then counts off the second number: 1, 2, *three*, then goes back to recount all: 1, 2, 3, 4, 5, 6, *seven*. Another more sophisticated and efficient example of "counting all," is when the child counts: 1, 2, 3, *four* then continues the count for three more: 5, 6, *seven*, to reach the total. When children choose to add this way without outside direction, they are working the problem out in a way that makes sense to them. An observant teacher watches "what makes sense to them" to determine how

complex their math thinking has become. Eventually, when children have formed an adequate knowledge base to support a more sophisticated, efficient and complex idea of "counting on" from the *four*, as in: *four* 5, 6, *seven*, they will do it. Teachers need not attempt to teach children this idea directly. When they do, children learn only superficial knowledge of memorized steps to get right answers, and worse, an opportunity for children to figure out useful strategies for themselves is missed.

One teacher I know told me about an LD child in her classroom who was busy working on a paper-and-pencil math quiz. She watched him in amazement, as he hit himself on the forehead moments before he wrote down his answer. As she walked up behind him to see what was going on, she heard him say to himself, as he inflicted yet another blow, "put *six* in my head, 7, 8, 9, 10, *eleven*" which he wrote down on his paper. The traditional lesson of informing children how to use the strategy of "counting on" had not been sufficient for this child. Not to be discouraged, his previous teacher had come up with an "imaginative," alternative method which the child was using to generate answers in the "approved way" on his quiz. Is the child "counting on" or not? Where does he fall on the continuum of evidence representing more sophisticated, efficient and complex mental adaptation? You can see how the evidence of mental growth quickly becomes obscured by teaching children to memorize techniques rather than allowing them to figure out or construct the solutions for themselves.

Let me contrast this example of "counting on" with another one observed in a constructivist math class. Sharon, a second grader, was given the problem of 92+9 to figure out in her head. The teacher observed her as she busily began to "count all" quietly to herself: 1, 2, 3, 4, 5, 6, 7, 8, 9, 10, 11, 12. Suddenly, Sharon hesitated and said, "Oh, darn!" She paused again before she murmured thoughtfully, "Let's see, 92..." And wagging her head to the count, she continued triumphantly, "93, 94, 95, 96, 97, 98, 99, 100, 101!" She had figured out by herself that "counting all" was an unnecessarily long process. Is there any doubt that she had constructed a "counting on" strategy for herself? What a shame it is that all children can't have the satisfying experience of constructing the idea of "counting on" for themselves! When children do this for themselves, their previous knowledge base grows, and they will be able to construct even more complex mathematical relationships.

Fortunately, there is plenty a teacher can do to support and encourage mental growth. The environment was very much a factor in Sharon's figuring out how to "count on." Sharon's teacher knew when to give her that difficult problem. Sharon's teacher also knew that it would not be long before Sharon figures out 92+9 by saying, "Well, I just take one off the 92 to make 91 and add nine to make 100 and then put the one back on to make 101." She will be ready for the SUPERMARKET GAME included in this chapter much sooner than children who are taught steps to obtain right answers.

Recently, I was watching two four-year-olds pretending to cook their dinner in the housekeeping corner. I listened intently as they discussed the weight of some play dough they had put into a balance scale. Pam busily inspected the dial and pronounced that "the hamburger weighs two pounds and a quarter." To this, JayeP replied, "I think it weighs two pounds and a nickel!" I tell this anecdote to illustrate once again how readily the previous knowledge base of children is revealed to those teachers who are listening and thinking about what children say and do. As Pam and JayeP go through the motions of measurement in their preschool setting, they are starting out on another continuum, one that is headed toward the construction of a more complete idea of measurement. What we teachers need to do is support all their thinking along the way so that a mature understanding of this concept, perhaps years from now, is realized.

Another point to consider is the young age at which children have experiences with and think about money. It's not surprising that JayeP knew more about money than about pounds. Do you have early memories of treats paid for with carefully counted coins? I remember how much one piece of bubble gum cost and one scoop of ice cream and one comic book. I remember that the tooth fairy brought my next door neighbor more money than I received for a tooth. Rich and poor, city and country children alike all seem to learn early that money has value, and they pay attention to money experiences. The early knowledge base that children build about money is information upon which ideas about number can be generalized. Consequently, money games may be especially relevant for children who are just learning about early number relationships.

GRAB FOR TREASURE is a good beginning game. Children take turns grabbing handfuls of a rice and coin mixture out of a shoe box. Very young children compare their "grabs" with the "grabs" of other players and construct ideas about more and less. It is usually someone who is motivated to "win" who will first figure out that counting the value of the pennies and nickels may be a better way to determine the winner than counting only the

number of coins in the "grab." Older children may play this game with game boards designed to categorize their coins and a new rule which allows for trading any unwanted coins. For example, when a player ends up with two quarters and a space for only one, listen for the level of logic, as the trade for the extra quarter is negotiated.

Children love to play ROLL THE PIGGY. The roll of two dice determines the number of pennies to be taken from the bank, and children can use a variety of strategies to make their play. They can match the number of pennies they take with the number of dots on each of the dice, *or* they can count the dots on the dice and then count out the same number of pennies, *or* they can count on from one die to the next, *or* they can add the numbers on the dice. The point is that children will be actively thinking no matter what level of thinking they use to play this game. They will take from their experience that which makes sense to them. And, the next time they play, it may be something different and more complex that they learn.

One of the most popular board games we developed was HURRAY, I LOST MY TOOTH! All the players begin with 10 lima bean "teeth" and try to collect the most money from the Tooth Fairy as they travel around the game board. Subtraction is such a hard idea for children who are still figuring out addition. A game about losing teeth emphasizes the remainder, without requiring subtraction to play. Many of the games in this chapter require the players to make change. Games such as MONEY WAR, SCHOOL DAYS, and ALEXANDER WHO USED TO BE RICH LAST SUNDAY nudge children even closer to subtraction thinking as they try to figure out which coins they need to equal a known total. That's a mental stretch for many young players.

THE SUPERMARKET GAME is a shopping board game in which players must "purchase" those items on which they land. If they land on a coupon, the value is deducted from the bill. We grew up with paper-and-pencil calculations so it's hard to imagine that young children can keep this tally going in their heads so much better than we can. Children who do not use paper and pencil construct amazing mental math abilities. A fourth grade teacher I know labored to get her students to do five or ten minutes of mental math (i.e., without paper and pencil) each day. Yet, the first and second graders who were never given paper and pencil could do mental math for an hour or longer. Some teachers may be tempted to allow calculators for this game because of the long list of calculations to be made, and because of their own experience with such lists. Of course, calculators will require much less thinking, but they could be useful to settle disputes of the children's final tallies. But, let the children suggest it!

$$$MONEY WAR$$$

Good Game for: Making change, addition, making comparisons, coin recognition

Of Interest for Ages: 6-9 years   **Number of Players:** 2

Materials Needed to Play: Money playing cards, "Bank" of coins

Make Your Own Materials: Remove carefully and laminate the money playing cards OR write comparible decimals on unlined, 3 1/2 x 5 inch index cards.

Setup to Play: Let children choose which coin cards they want to use (e.g., 2 pennies and 2 nickels *or* 2 nickels and 2 dimes, *or* 2 nickels, 2 dimes and 1 quarter *or* equivalent decimals). Deal the chosen cards evenly into two stacks. Place one stack face down in front of each player, as in regular War.

Game Rules:
1. Each player turns over the top card. Whichever player's card has the highest monetary value, that player gets the amount of money designated from the bank.
2. The played game cards are put to one side, and the players turn up the next cards.
3. When the top cards are of the same value, there is no play.
4. Play continues until the players use all of their cards.

Object of the Game: To have the most money after all the cards have been played.

Game Variations: A third person can play by being the banker. The banker plays the winner and the loser becomes the banker. The game can also be played by adding the value of both cards to determine how much is taken from the bank by the player of the winning card. Often the children will "adjust" the rules to their level of understanding. For example, younger children playing with the cards alone may count their money cards as one point per card rather than score the cards according to their monetary value. This is fine. They will invent a more complex system as they are capable of conceptualizing one. By letting the children figure out the scoring for themselves, they will construct a better understanding for the relationships involved, and the teacher will learn about their development from observing.

Game History: Adapted from an original game by Courtney Waterfield Saintsing, 1st-grade teacher at John B. Dey Elementary School in Virginia Beach, VA.

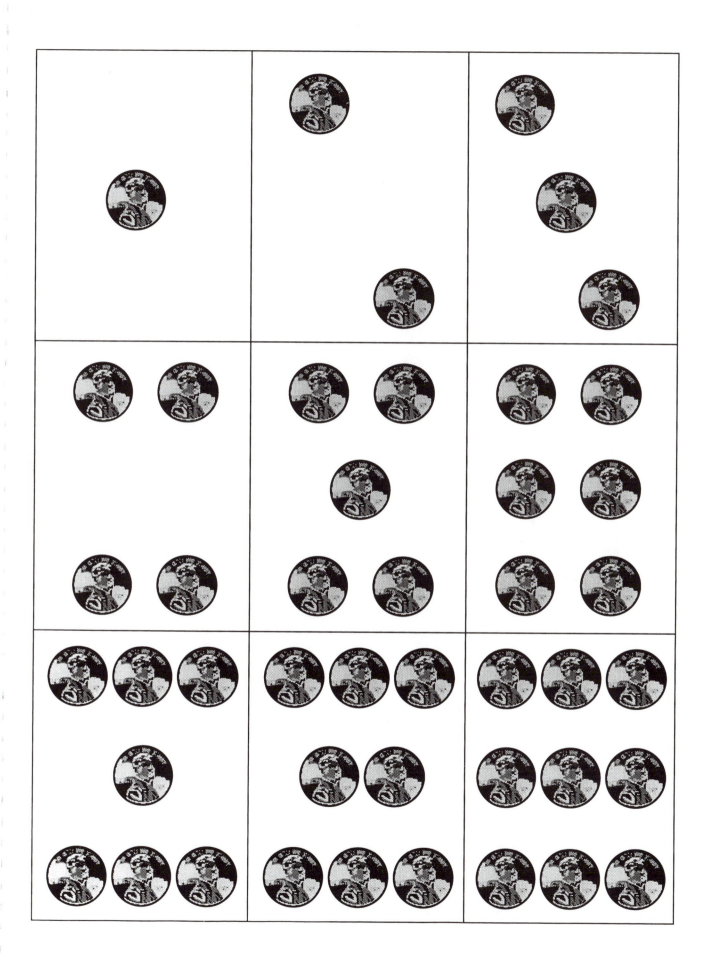

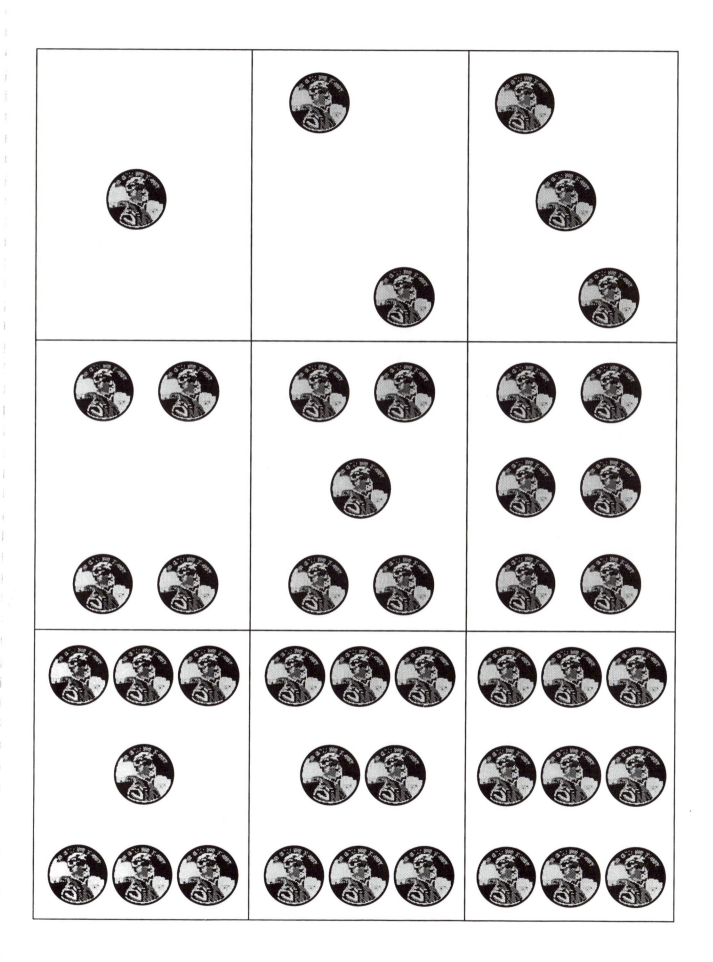

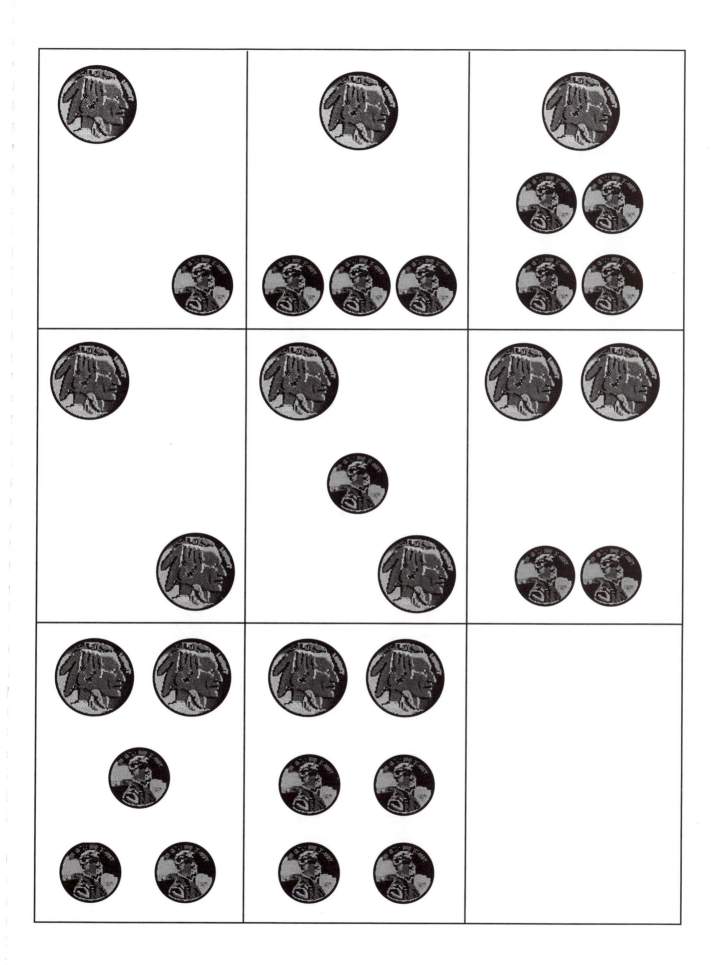

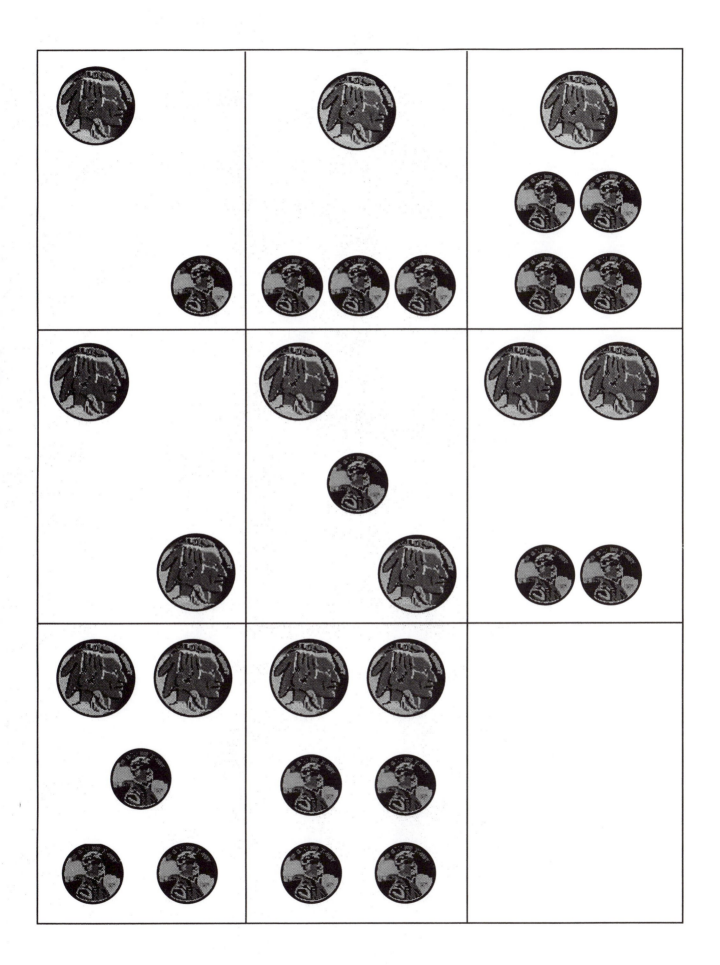

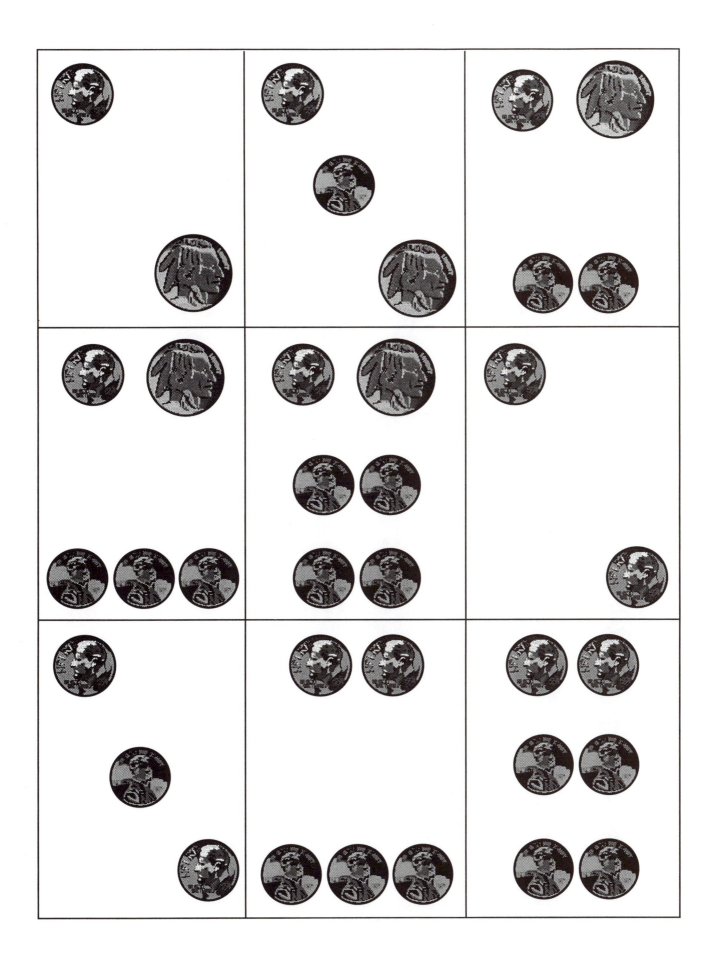

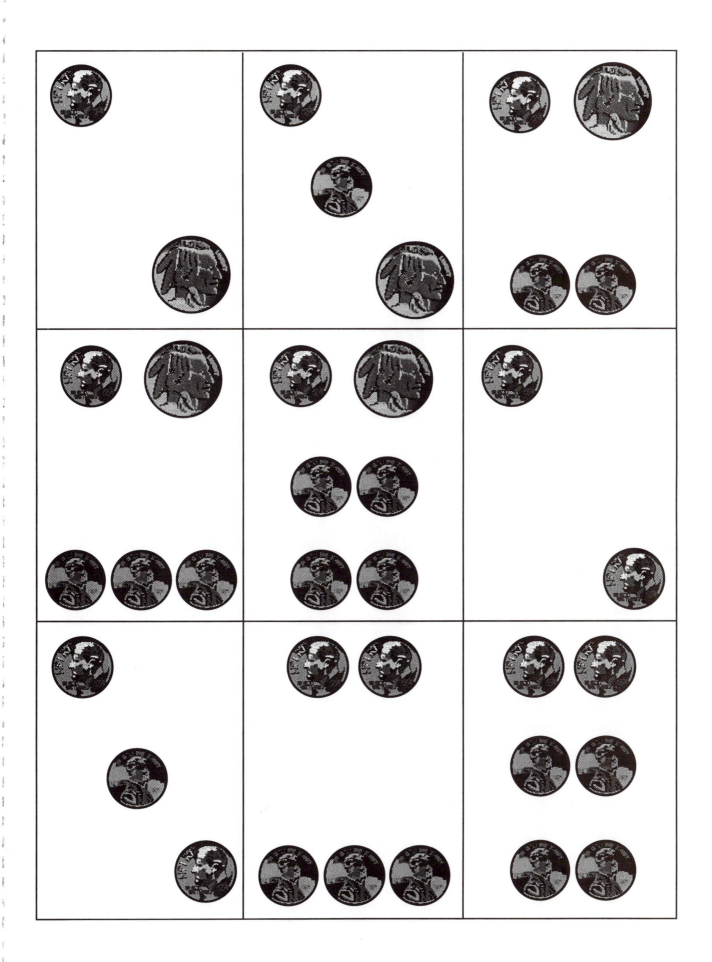

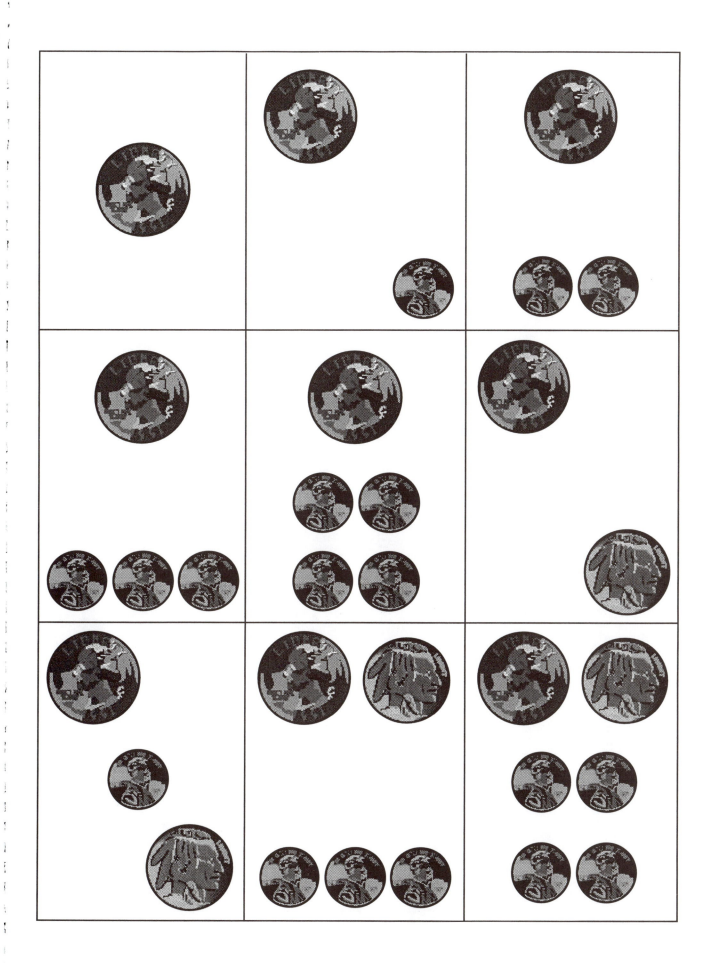

$$$SCHOOL DAYS$$$

Good Game for: Making change, addition, counting, coin recognition

Of Interest for Ages: 6-9 years   **Number of Players:** 2-4

Materials Needed to Play: School Days Game Board and game cards, "bank" of coins and bills, 2 dice, 2-4 game markers

Make Your Own Materials: Remove carefully and assemble, taping together from the back, the four corner sections of the School Days game board. Color the game board, then laminate. Laminate and cut apart the game cards.

Setup to Play: Players may choose a banker or act as their own. Each player starts with 3 one-dollar bills, 1 half dollar, 2 quarters, 5 dimes, 4 nickels, and 4 pennies. Let the children decide to play with dice with dots *or* numerals *or* one of each.

Game Rules:
1. Roll the dice to see who goes first. Play moves clockwise from player to player around the board.
2. "Allowance" is $.25 and is collected from the bank every time a player lands on or passes an "Allowance" space. If the player lands directly *on* the space, he or she also draws a card.
3. If card directs player to go backward, turn concludes after play even if player lands on "Draw a card" or "Allowance."
4. The first player to finish rolls the dice to get a "Lucky Number." From this point, when anyone rolls the "Lucky Number," he or she must pay the first player to finish $.20.

Object of the Game: To move around the game board and be the player with the most money at the end of the game.

Game Variations: The game board can be made easier or harder by changing the money values on the game board and cards. When children act as their own bankers, there will be more mental engagement, as everyone watches to ensure accurate accounting.

Game History: Adapted from an original game by Courtney Waterfield Saintsing, 1st-grade teacher at John B. Dey Elementary School in Virginia Beach, VA.

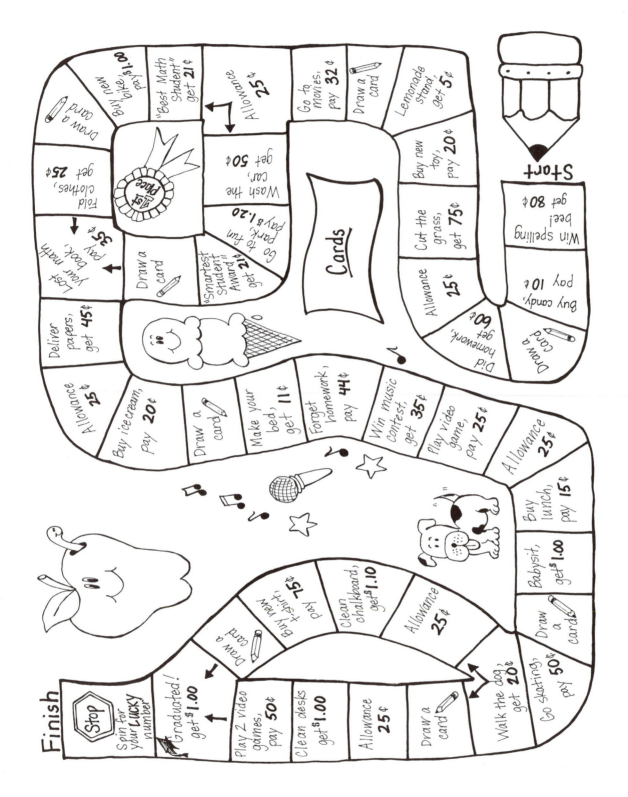

The gameboard should look like this when assembled.

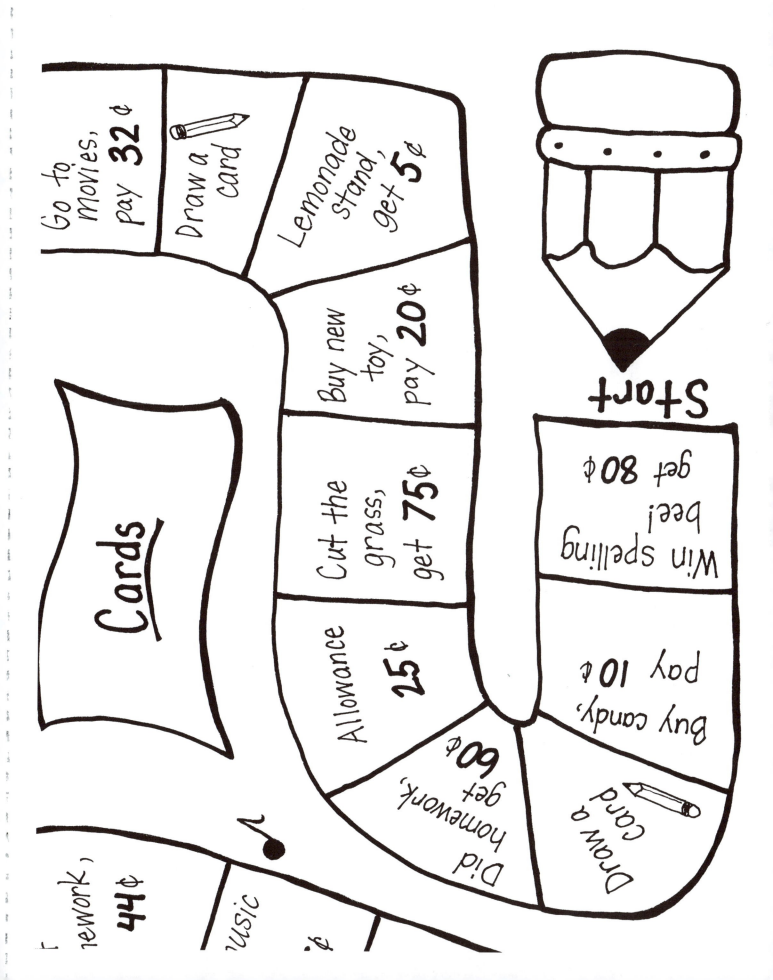

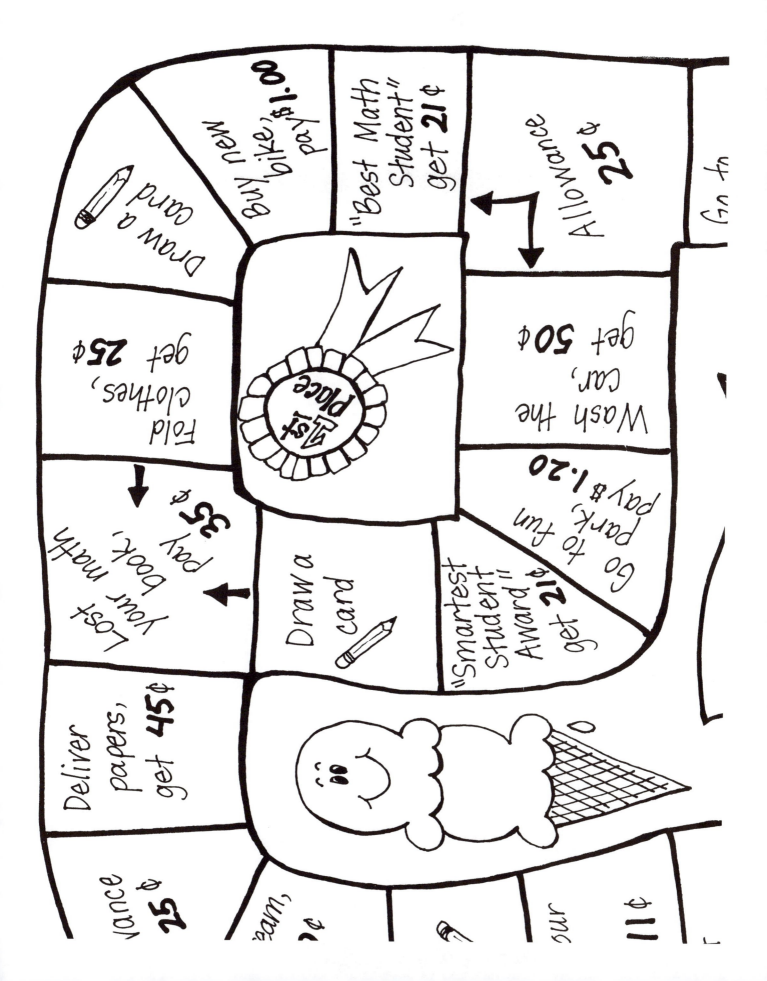

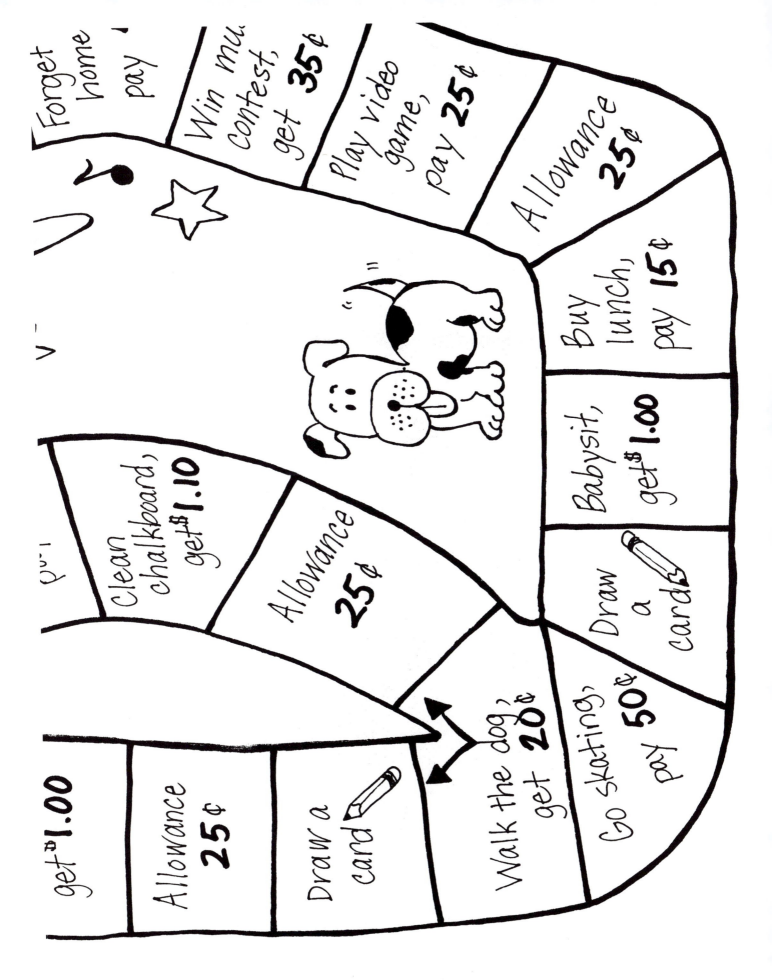

Allowa **2**

Buy ice crea
Pay **20¢**

Draw a
card

Make you
bed,
get **11**

Emmet

Finish

Stop

Spin for
your *LUCKY*
number

Graduated!
get **$1.00**

Buy new
t-shirt,
pay **75¢**

Draw
a
card

Play 2 video
games,
pay **50¢**

Clean desks
get **$1.00**

Stay home from school. Lose a turn.	Great student! Get $1.00 from the bank.	Pay everyone 10¢.
Dog ate homework! Pay the bank 20¢.	Move ahead 3 spaces.	Move back 2 spaces.
Move another player ahead 2 spaces!	Helped your teacher! Roll Again!	Did your homework! Get 30¢ from the bank.

Roll Again!	Everyone pays you 5¢.	Move another player back 1 space.
Good Grades! Roll Again!	Happy Student! Move ahead 1 space.	Came to school! Move ahead 2 spaces.
Late to school! Move back 3 spaces.	Early to school! Get 20¢ from the bank.	Stayed up late. Lose a turn.

$$$HURRAY, I LOST MY TOOTH!$$$

Good Game for: Making change, addition, counting, coin recognition

Of Interest for Ages: 5-7 years   **Number of Players:** 2-4

Materials Needed to Play: Tooth game board and game cards, 20-40 "teeth,"
                              2-4 game markers, Tooth Fairy "bank" of coins,
                              small box for "teeth," 2 dice

Make Your Own Materials: Assemble, taping together from the back, the four corner sections of the Tooth game board found on the following four pages. Color the game board to suit, then laminate. Game cards can be laminated and cut apart. Dried lima beans work very well as "teeth," as they are flat and do not roll around.

Setup to Play: Each player begins the game with ten teeth and one game marker. Let the children decide whether to play with dice with dots *or* numerals *or* one of each.

Game Rules:
1. Players roll the dice to determine order of play. Play moves clockwise.
2. The first player rolls the dice and moves his or her game marker according to the roll. If the player lands on a tooth, he or she "loses" a tooth, picks a game card and follows the directions on the card. Teeth are left in a small box and money is collected from the Tooth Fairy bank.
3. The game ends when one player loses all ten teeth.
4. Players all count their money to see who the winner is.

Object of the Game: To move around the game board, and receive the most money from the Tooth Fairy bank by the time the first player loses all ten teeth.

Game Variations: By using pictures of teeth along with words on the game cards, children who are not yet readers will be able to play. Likewise, the coin pictures used along with numbers to depict the money left by the Tooth Fairy offer more help for children who can find a quarter and two pennies but can not yet find $.27. The game board can be made harder by taping decimals over the coin pictures.

Game History: Adapted from an original game by Susan Gilles, kindergarten teacher at Harding Academy, Nashville, TN.

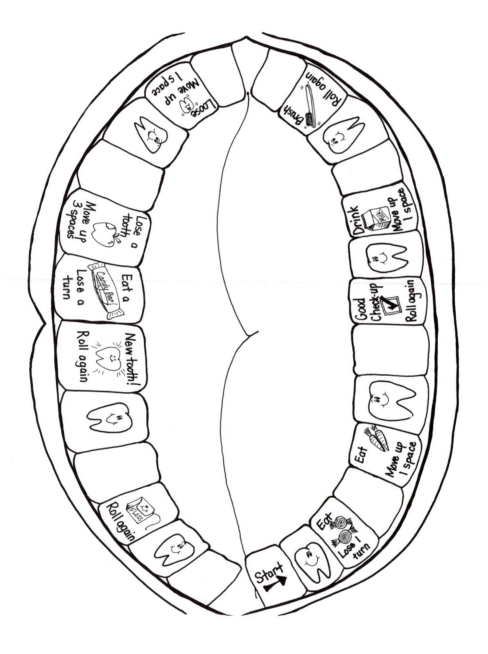

The gameboard should look like this when assembled.

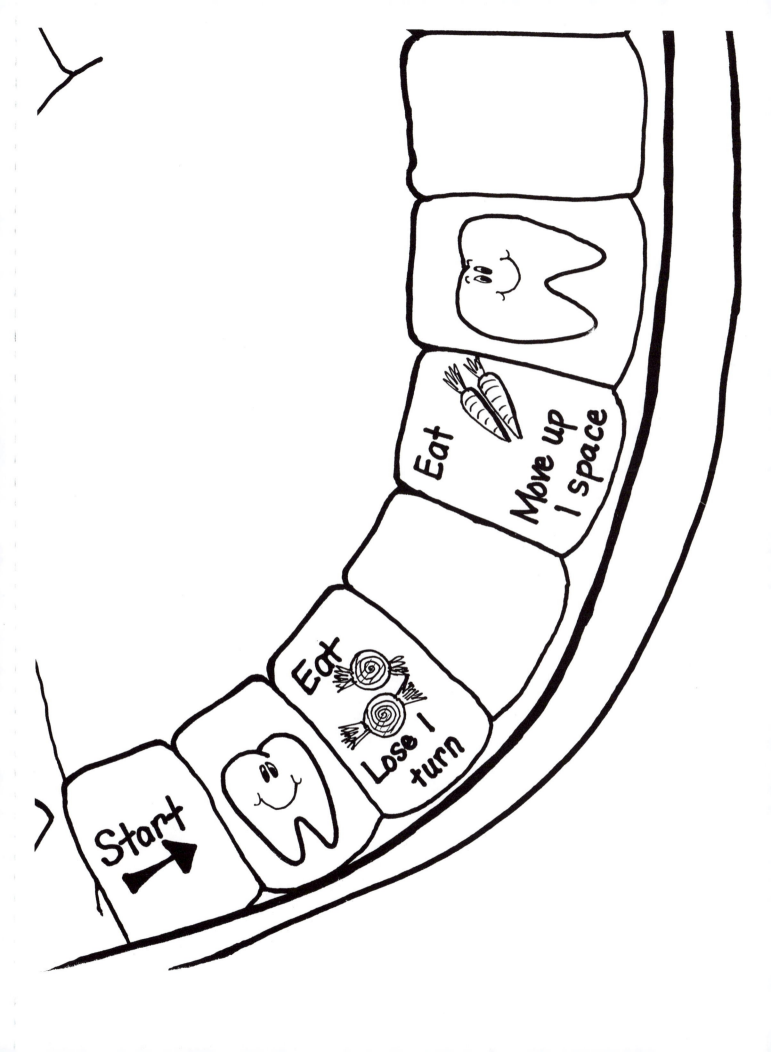

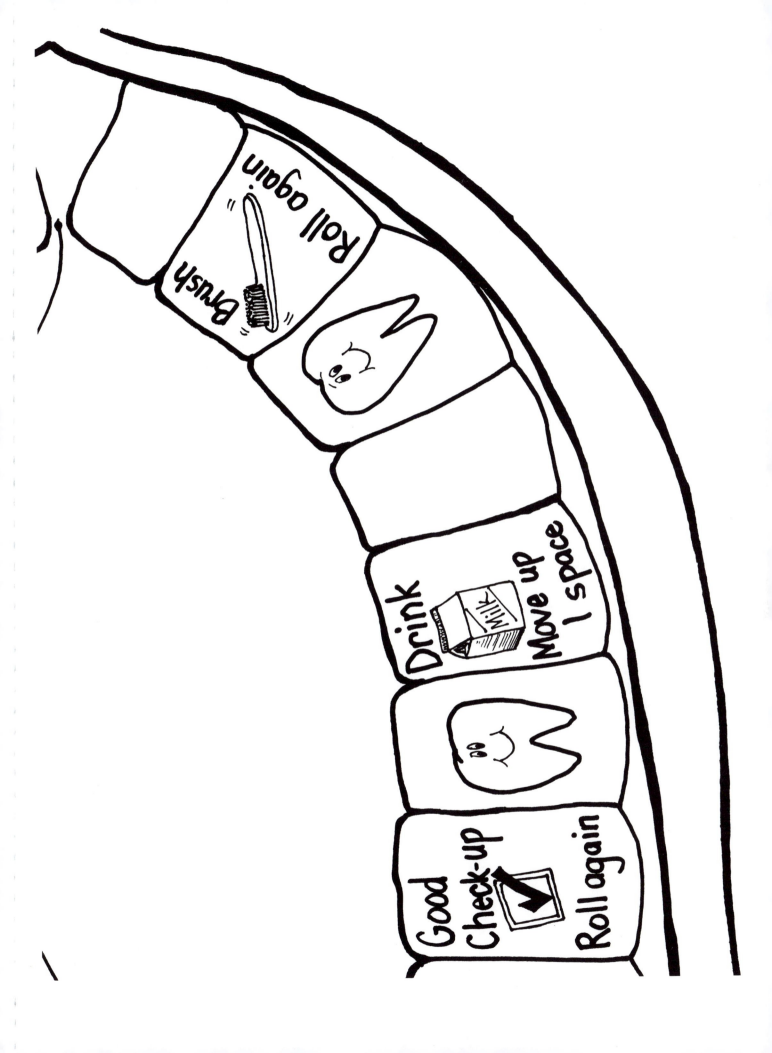

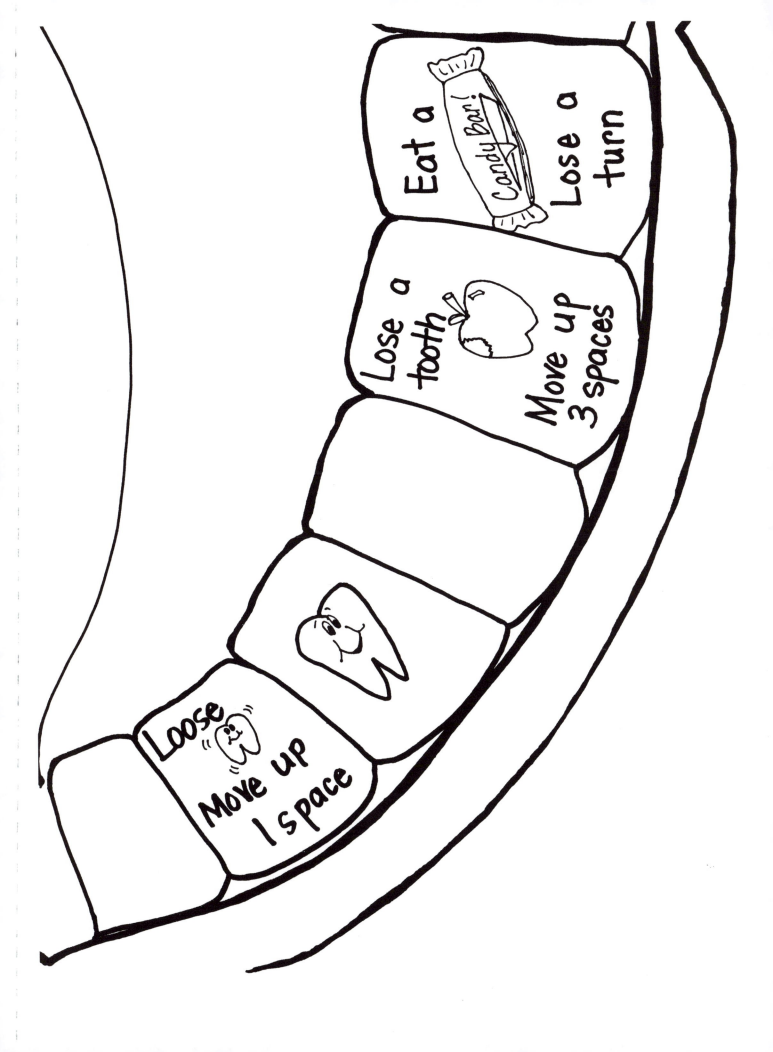

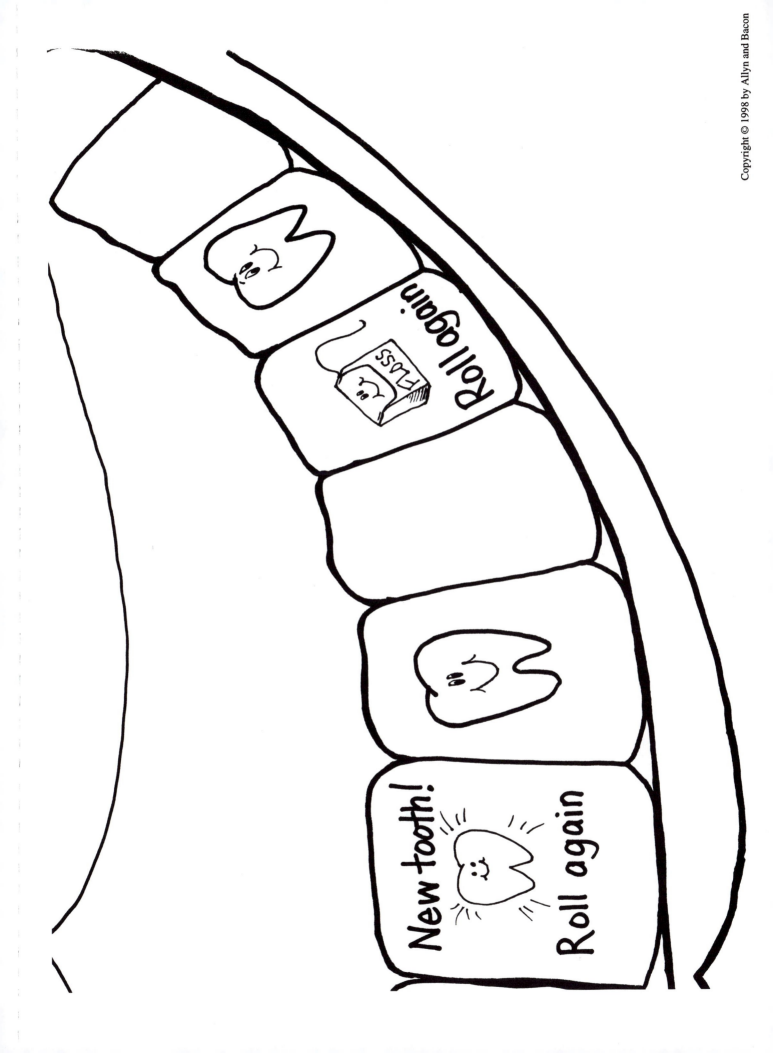

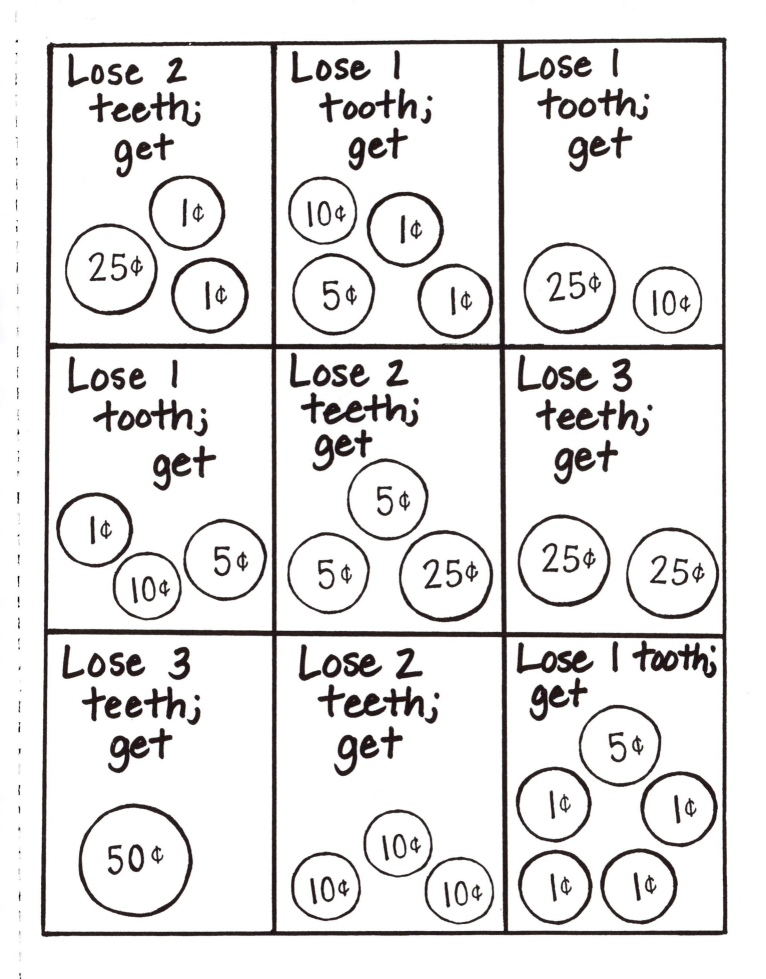

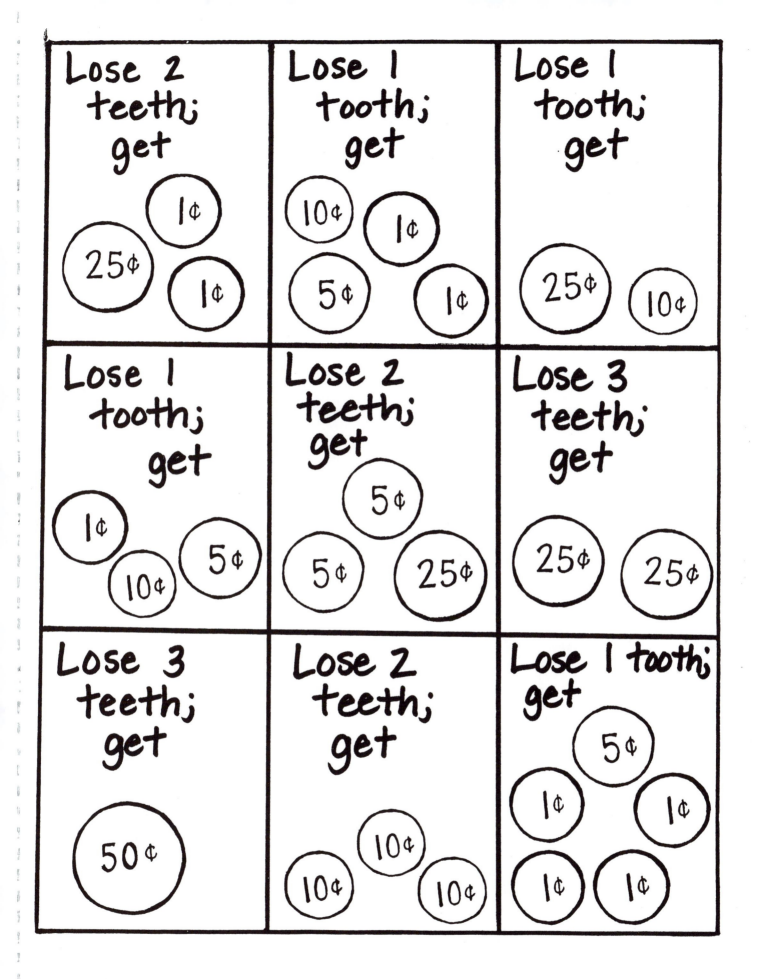

Lose 2 teeth; get	Lose 1 tooth; get	Lose 1 tooth; get
1¢ 25¢ 1¢	10¢ 1¢ 5¢ 1¢	25¢ 10¢
Lose 1 tooth; get	Lose 2 teeth; get	Lose 3 teeth; get
1¢ 10¢ 5¢	5¢ 5¢ 25¢	25¢ 25¢
Lose 3 teeth; get	Lose 2 teeth; get	Lose 1 tooth; get
50¢	10¢ 10¢ 10¢	5¢ 1¢ 1¢ 1¢ 1¢

ALEXANDER. . .
WHO USED TO BE RICH LAST SUNDAY

Good Game for: Making change, addition, counting, coin recognition

Of Interest for Ages: 6-9 years   **Number of Players:** 2-4

Materials Needed to Play: Alexander Game Board and cards, 2-4 playing pieces, spinner, "bank" of coins and bills

Make Your Own Materials: Assemble, taping together from the back, the four corner sections of the game board found on the following four pages. Color the game board to suit, then laminate. Game cards can be laminated and cut apart. The game spinner can be incorporated onto the game board. Use a brass fastener to attach a large paper clip or snap a commercially available spinner onto the center of the dial.

Set-up to Play: Each player begins with 3 quarters, 1 dime, 2 nickels, and 5 pennies.

Game Rules:
1. Players spin to determine order of play. Play moves clockwise around the board.
2. The first player spins the spinner and moves accordingly. If the player lands on a space with coins, that amount is collected from the bank. Bus token spaces require player to pay bank $.15 and lose next turn. Landing on any of the spaces with pictures means player picks a game card and follows the directions on the card. Landing on a Walkie Talkie requires player to give one dollar to the bank.
3. When the first player circles game board, the game is over and players count their money to determine the winner.

Object of the Game: To have the most money by the time the first player circles the game board and game is completed.

Game Variations: For older children tape over the rebuses and coin pictures with words and numerals on game board and cards.

Game History: Inspired by Judith Viorst's story of <u>Alexander Who Used to be Rich Last Sunday</u>, and adapted from an original game by Becky Alexander who teaches 2nd grade at Butts Road Primary in Chesapeake, VA.

The gameboard should look like this when assembled.

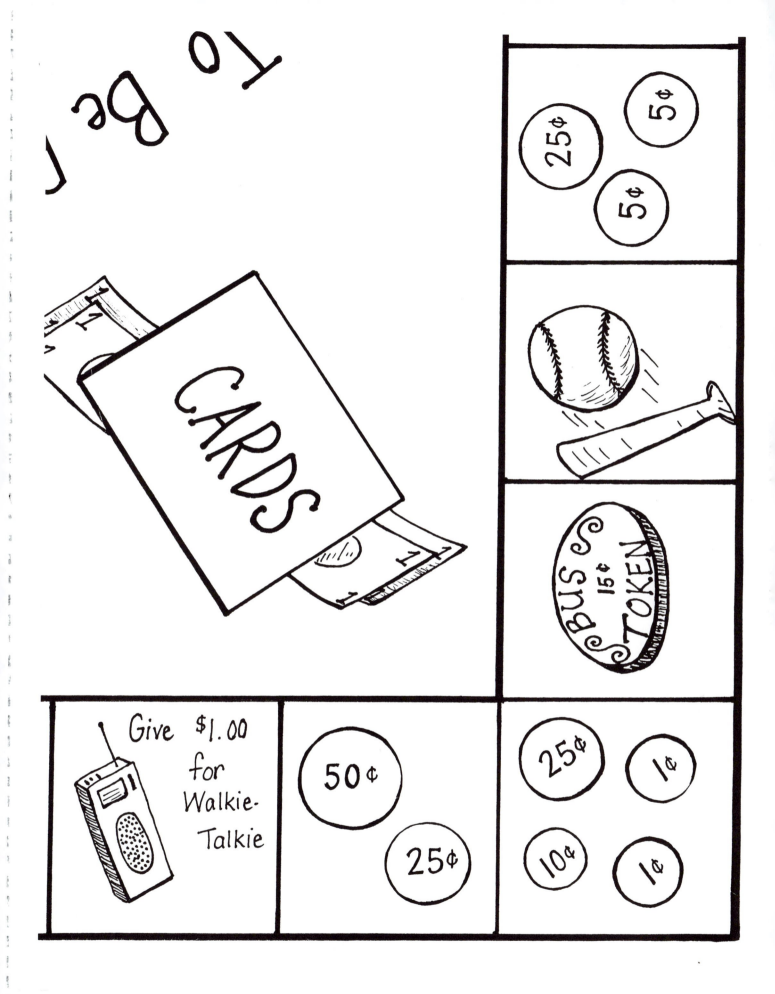

Who Used It, $ Alexander's $

Spin Again

2

7

Move 2 Spaces, Spin Again

10¢ 10¢ 10¢ 10¢ 10¢

25¢ 25¢ 25¢

Give $1.00 for Walkie-Talkie

BUS 15¢ TOKEN

Alexander was showing off by juggling two dimes, one nickel, and a penny. They all fell and **some** rolled into the drain. Good-bye 6¢	Playing kickball next to Mom's flower garden was **not** a good idea! Now Mom's favorite rose bush is broken. Good-bye 75¢	Alexander went to the phone booth at Pearson's store. **Yeah!** He found some money! Hello 25¢ ☺
Oh... how **WONDERFUL** ... Grandma has come for another visit! You know what **that** means! Hello $1.00 ☺	Alexander just bought 10 pieces of red licorice at Mr. Bulky's. (It was **only** 1¢ each.) Good-bye 10¢	Alexander buys some used X-Men comics from Leo. He is **only** charging 3¢ for each one! Good-bye 9¢
Ooops... it just slipped out! Alexander has to pay a fine for calling his brother a name again. Good-bye 25¢	Alexander lost a tooth! The Tooth Fairy left him a nice present. Hello 50¢ ☺	Alexander's money was used for a magic trick. The trick **didn't** work. Good-bye 8¢

Alexander buys two pieces of gum at 5¢ each. Good-bye 10¢	Oh **JOY!** Grandma has come for a visit! You know what **that** means! Hello $1.00 ☺	Alexander just ate his brother's candy bar and Nicholas is upset. Alexander **must** pay him back! Good-bye 28¢
Alexander rented out some of his toys. He rented his wagon and scooter for an hour. Hello 15¢ ☺	Alexander really wants a special X-Men comic book. He just **has** to have it! Good-bye 30¢	Want to buy a deck of cards? Alexander did, and now he is **sorry**. Good-bye 32¢
Alexander made another bet with Anthony! And he **lost**! Good-bye 25¢	Alexander's dad taught him **not** to call people names. Now Alexander has to pay a fine for his unkind words! Good-bye 30¢	Alexander was able to rent out his roller skates for two hours! Hello 12¢ ☺

Alexander took empty bottles and got the deposit money. Hello 35¢	Alexander has **always** liked Eddie's snake. Eddie will now rent it for 6¢ an hour. Good-bye 18¢	Alexander sells hot chocolate to the ice skaters. That's 5¢ a cup. Hello 40¢
Alexander **lost** two of his brother's pencils. Nicholas wants the money to buy new ones. Good-bye 16¢	At the garage sale Alexander bought a melted candle! **What** will he do with **that**? Good-bye 7¢	Alexander just **had** to have some more gum. He bought three pieces at 5¢ each. Good-bye 15¢
Would **you** like a glass of lemonade? Get it from Alexander! Only 3¢ a glass. Hello 33 ¢	Alexander just **had** to have that bear that was missing one eye! (He should stay **away** from garage sales.) Good-bye 35¢	Alexander made a bet with his older brother. And he lost. Good-bye 50¢

$$$THE SUPERMARKET GAME$$$

Good Game for: Addition and subtraction of money (decimals)

Of Interest for Ages: 8-10 years   **Number of Players:** 2-4

Materials Needed to Play: Supermarket Game Board and cards, 2-4 game markers, blank cover cards, one die or spinner

Make Your Own Materials: Assemble the game board pieces according to arrows and tape together from the back. Color the supermarket aisle with one color to indicate the game path. Color the rest of the game board and laminate. Laminate and cut apart the game cards. Make a set of blank cover cards with blank index cards.

Set-up to Play: Match the game cards to the same $$ value on the game board. (E.g., in aisle #1, banana game card $1.30 would be placed on top of game board space #2 with the same picture.)

Game Rules:
1. Roll the die to determine who goes first. Play moves clockwise around the board.
2. Each player rolls the die and moves his or her game marker accordingly. A player lands on a space, takes the card showing what must be paid for groceries there, then closes the space to further play by covering it with a blank card. The players add up the cards they accumulate representing their grocery bills. If a player lands on a space denoting a *coupon*, that amount is subtracted from the player's cumulative bill. If a player lands on *free sample*, the player gets an extra turn. If player lands on *clean up*, he or she loses a turn.
3. Play proceeds down one aisle and up the next until all players reach the checkout.
4. Players total their bills, and whoever has spent the least amount of money wins.

Object of the Game: To checkout with the lowest grocery bill.

Game Variations: This is a challenging game especially if children are not figuring out problems in their head every day. The $$ cards serve as a way to prove the bill if another player challenges the tally. Calculators can be used for a final check.

Game History: Adapted from an original game by Jennifer A. Johnson, teacher-in-training at Old Dominion University, Norfolk, VA.

Welcome!

Start Shopping →

Thank You, Come Again!

Finish! (Cashier)

Clean Up!

Free Sample!

Coupon Save 75¢ today! 75¢

Coupon Save 50¢ today! 50¢

Apple	$0.99
Bananas	$1.30
Grapes	$2.99
Oranges	$0.90
Carrots	$1.25
Mushrooms	$0.56
Broccoli	$1.49
Bread	$0.99
Paper Towels	$1.73
Taco	$1.46
Soy Sauce	$1.85
Noodles	$0.35
Peanut Butter	$3.00
Fruit Snacks	$3.35
Pie	$3.00
Cookies	$1.05
Oil	$0.86
Flour	$0.59
Salt & Pepper	$4.21
Jam	$3.59
Hot Cocoa	$2.01
Apple Sauce	$0.69
Soup	$1.19
Ketchup	$0.89
Beans	$2.10
Chips	$0.99
Chocolate	$0.27
Popsicle	$0.35
Apple	$1.23
Milk	$1.59
Eggs	$1.99
Toothpaste	$3.36

The gameboard should look like this when assembled.

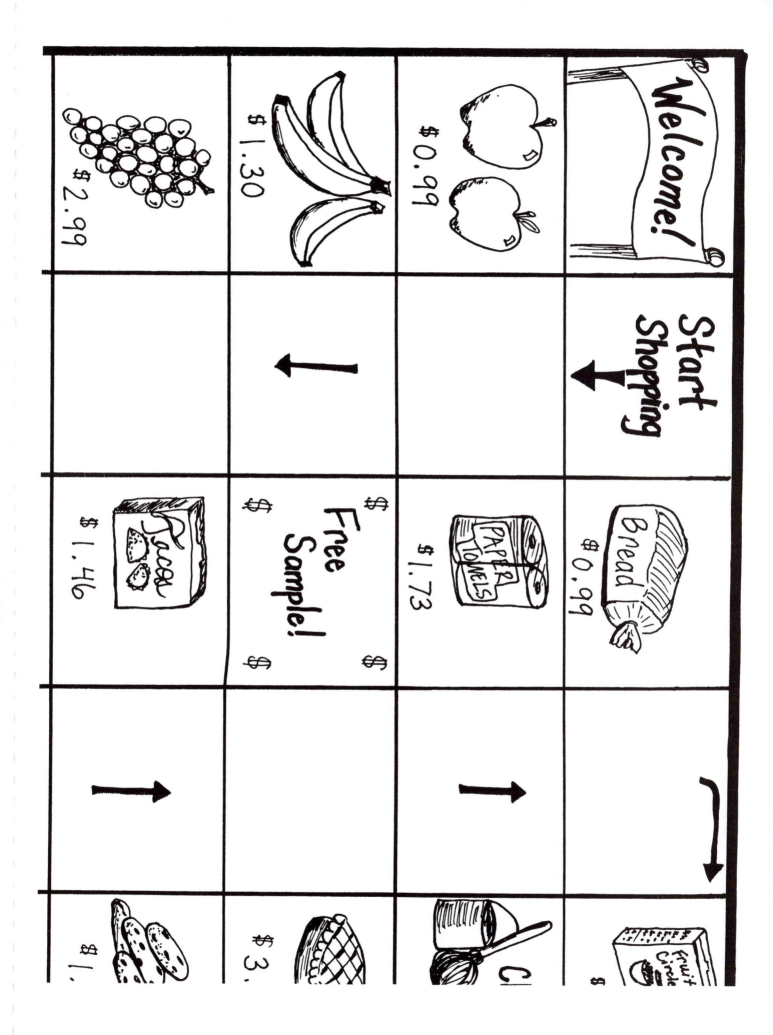

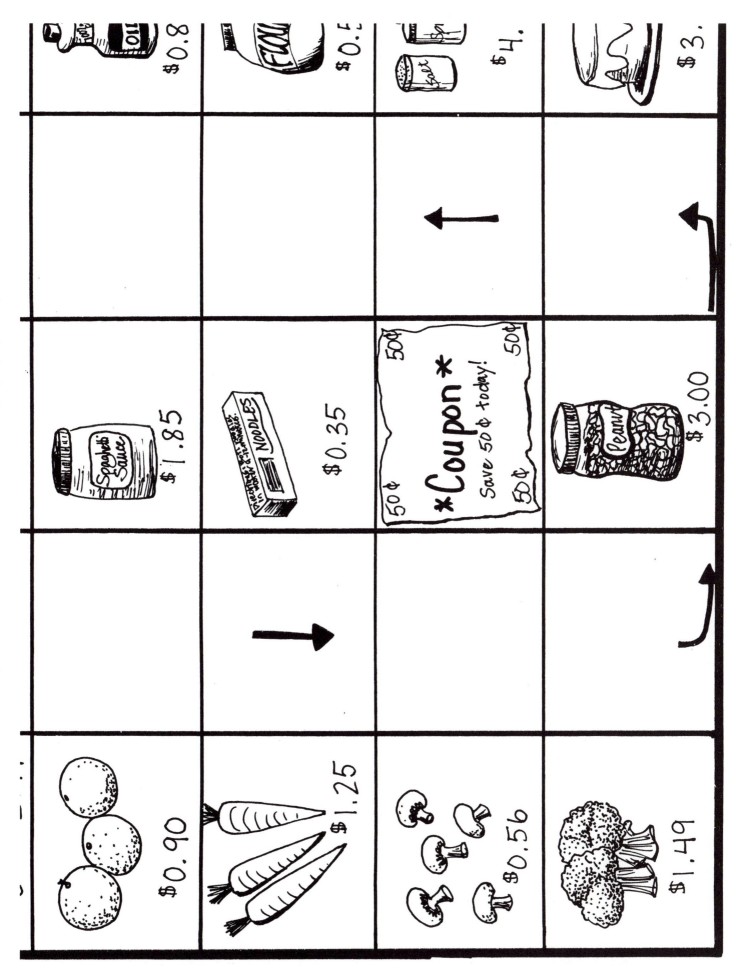

$0.8

$0.5

$4.

$3.

$1.85

$0.35

Coupon

Save 50¢ today!

50¢   50¢

50¢   50¢

$3.00

$0.90

$1.25

$0.56

$1.49

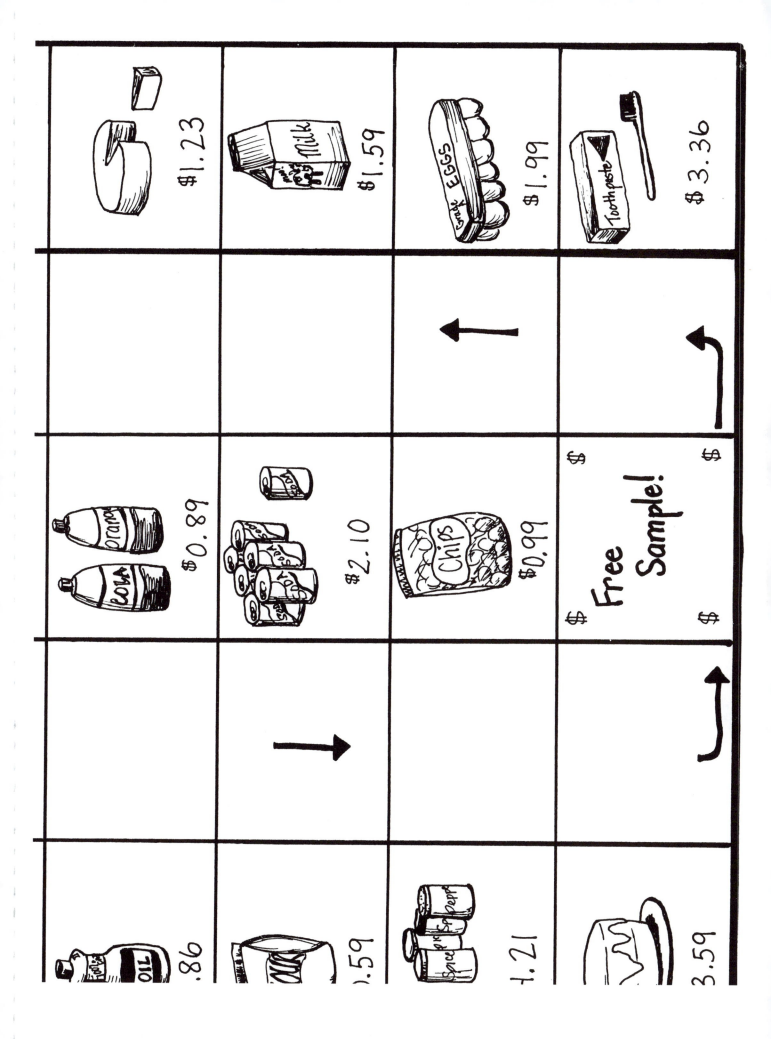

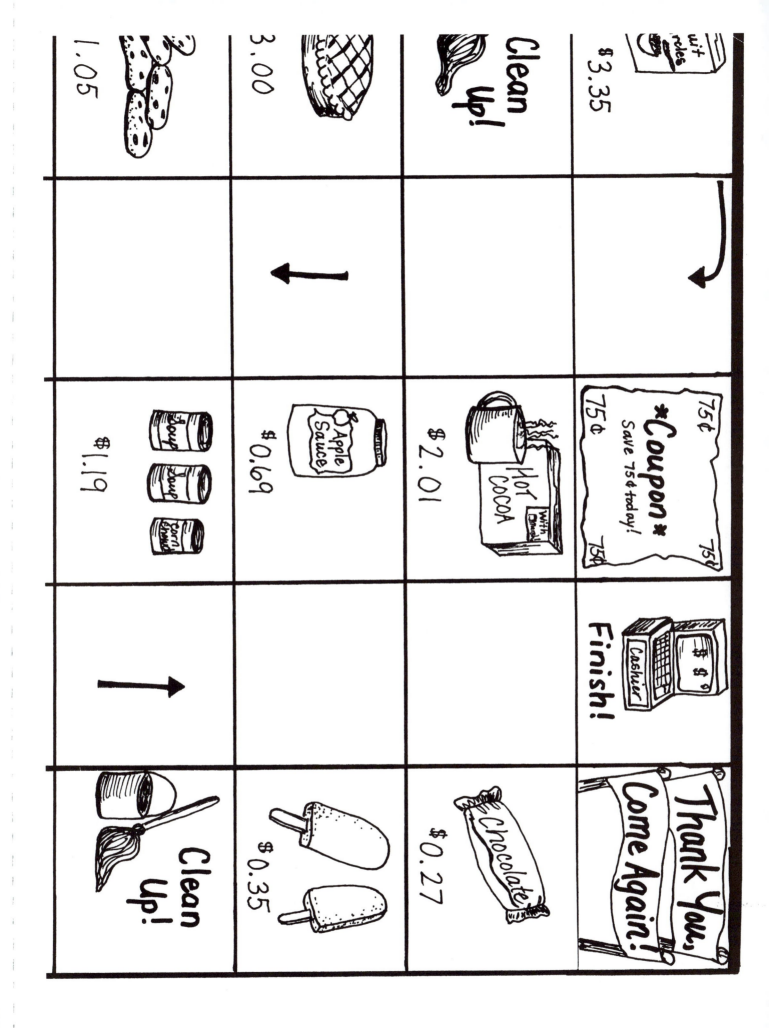

$0.56

$1.49

FLOUR $0.59

SODA $2.10

NOODLES $0.35

Salt Spice Pepper $4.21

Chips $0.99

50¢   50¢
Coupon
Save 50¢ today!
50¢   50¢

$3.59

$ $
Free
Sample!
$ $

Peanut $3.00

$$$GRAB FOR TREASURE$$$

Good Game for: Addition, counting, coin recognition

Of Interest for Ages: 5-7 years   **Number of Players:** 2-3

Materials Needed to Play: Plastic shoe box with lid, 5 pounds of rice,
real or plastic play coins

Make Your Own Materials: Although a plastic shoe box with an airtight lid makes a better long-term storage container for rice, a cardboard shoe box could be used temporarily.

Setup to Play: Mix rice and coins in shoe box. See illustration on page 94.

Game Rules:
1. Each player grabs one handful of rice-coin mixture.
2. Player with the most coins or the most value goes first. Watch how the children figure out their own scoring system.
3. First player grabs one handful of rice-coin mixture and places his or her handful in the lid to separate coins from rice. Player keeps coins and returns rice to the shoe box.
4. Play continues clockwise until all players grab handfuls of rice with no coins for two consecutive turns.
5. Children figure out the winner by counting numbers of coins *or* total value of coins.

Object of the Game: To grab the most coins *or* the most value.

Game Variations: Young children often count number of coins rather than the value of the coins in money games. Teachers will learn more about how children construct money relationships if they watch this process rather than direct it.

Game History: Adapted from a traditional party game by Elizabeth Wells, a kindergarten teacher at Merrimack Elementary School in Hampton, VA.

$$$ROLL THE PIGGY$$$

Good Game For: Money recognition, counting, addition

Of Interest for Ages: 5-7 years   **Number of Players:** 2-4

Materials Needed to Play: Piggy-dice-roller, 2 or 3 dice, 2-4 small piggy banks, "bank" of pennies, kitchen timer

Make Your Own Materials: Make your own Piggy-dice-roller out of a two-quart plastic juice bottle, as shown. Pink felt can be attached with a hot glue gun. The small piggy banks for individual players can be made by stapling paper pigs to the sides of cups with resealable lids. Add slots in each lid to complete the banks. Real pennies are cheaper than plastic pennies. Borrow a kitchen timer with a dinger.

Set-up to Play: Children sit on the floor around the "bank" of pennies with enough space

to roll the Piggy-dice-roller between them. Insert two or three dice through the "snout." Individual piggy banks are placed in front of each player.

Game Rules:
1. Each player rolls the piggy-dice-roller to determine who rolls first.
2. To begin play, the first player rolls the piggy-dice-roller to the player to his or her left. That player's score is calculated from the dice and that amount in pennies is taken from the game bank and placed into that player's individual piggy bank.
3. Play continues clockwise until the timer goes off in three to five minutes.
4. The winner is the player with the most pennies.

Object of the Game: To have the most pennies before the timer goes off.

Game Variations: The children can choose whether they want dice with dots or with numerals or a combination. Young children who are just learning to add can eliminate the timer and use two dice with dots and count to get their totals. More experienced children can add numerals to get their totals. Others may want to add the two dice with numerals then "count on" the die with dots to get the total. Teachers can watch as children construct these number relationships for themselves.

Game History: Adapted from an original classroom game by Jan Oyster, a kindergarten teacher at Great Bridge Primary School in Chesapeake, VA.

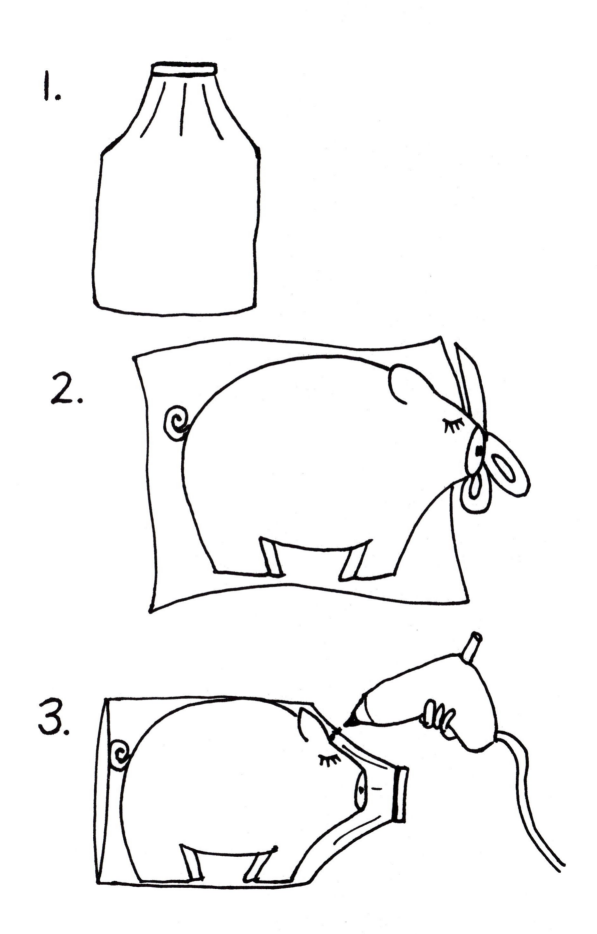

CHAPTER 5

THINKING ON YOUR FEET

"Education is not the filling of a pail, but the lighting of a fire."
- William Butler Yeats

Most teachers will *say* individualizing instruction is important, but do they *do* it? One of the biggest differences I have noticed between constructivist and traditional classroom teachers is in their perceived need to attend to individual students. Teachers who already have lessons planned for the next several weeks, who have an "adopted" curriculum to follow and workbooks for their students to complete, have little incentive to find out what their students can or really want to do. There is no need. Their plans are ready and their students better be. The emphasis for these teachers is on teacher production not on student input and choice. Constructivist teachers know that determining the interests and experience base of individual students is basic to good teaching. That is where they begin. And, when teachers begin at the beginning, they are more likely to provide the appropriate environment needed to support the mental and social growth of their students.

Bette Davis said that growing old is not for sissies. I would add, neither is constructivist teaching. Somedays it feels like a very steep, uphill climb. What can constructivist teachers do when they find themselves teaching in a traditional school surrounded by colleagues, who, as I've just described, are teaching by the book? Many schools require teachers to determine if the children have learned their math "facts" and other math objectives during the past nine-week period so they can come up with an appropriate "grade." Because of their inclination to be "kid-watchers," constructivist teachers ought to be able to play this requirement of assessing their students to everyone's satisfaction. For example, as children play the games described in this book, the teacher can observe to see which math relationships the children have committed to memory (i.e., know without pausing to think) and which ones they still must figure out. I know a kindergarten teacher who uses games and real-life problems exclusively for math but is required to provide "hard evidence" when it comes to the evaluation of each child. The "proof" of learning her principal requires are worksheet scores! This teacher knows from her day-to-day observations when her children can name all the numerals and what they represent. She knows when her students have memorized their so-called number "facts." She "tests" them *only* when she knows they know what the school expects them to learn, and she uses the required worksheets. When the children "perform" to the standard, the principal and parents are delighted, and the teacher puts away the worksheets until the next nine-week grading period.

I recommend another strategy which will encourage you, as well as garner support for your constructivist math classroom. After you have been teaching math by using math games and real-life problems for about two months, hold a math game open-house for your students' families. Be prepared for a *mob*. They will come in droves, and they won't want to leave. One group of five teachers I know instituted a change to constructivist math. Two months into the school year, they joined forces to sponsor an evening of math games for the families of their students. They booked the library, laid out their colorful gameboards and waited to see what would happen. They were unprepared for the response. Eighty percent of the children came with at least one parent. Some came with parents, siblings and grandparents! The library was not nearly large enough, so they quickly

divided up and went back to their separate classrooms. It was a wonderful night with children and parents sitting in groups all over the rooms playing the games. What was meant to be only an hour of math games turned into a whole evening of game playing with an unconditional and unified response of parental support for this new approach to teaching math. One older sibling expressed the spirit of the evening, as he reluctantly got up to leave, "Oh, Cookie, you're so-o-o luc-k-e-e-ey!!!"

Find a kindred spirit with the same constructivist philosophy and get together to offer one another support and solve mutual problems. Five teachers with this philosophy and one principal who trusts his or her teachers in a single elementary school can "rock the boat" sufficiently to bring about change in the whole school. I've seen it happen where I live, and I know it's happening in isolated elementary schools all over the country.

The games in this chapter need a lot of space and can be played outside. They involve plenty of action, both mentally and bodily. It seems to me that these games may be especially useful in situations where children have not had many opportunities to interact in game play and/or where there is the traditional expectation for a quiet classroom. Take the children outside during their regular recess time and bring along one of the games to play. Introduce game play for the first time in a setting where it is permissible to laugh and skip and interact and think without constraint. Make sure all the children have an opportunity to experience several of the games before you propose indoor games. If you have to work within the quiet classroom model, present this problem to the children to solve. Tell your students that you have some inside games that are fun to play, but you do not know what to do about the noise when the school expectation is for a quiet classroom. They'll eagerly promise they won't make any noise, of course. "But," you will say, "what if someone forgets and lets out an uncontrolled "whoop" of glee, as you have with these outdoor games?" "Then," they will say, "we'll need to find games that can be played more quietly." "Maybe we could try one or two," you will say, "and see what happens." When the teacher and the children work together this way to find solutions to classroom problems, children are more likely to understand the reason for their solution choices and will have a vested interest in making them work out. When children figure out solutions to problems for themselves, they construct a rationale to support their solution. The rationale acts as an internal guide which assists them as they conform to the requirements of their own solution. There is an added benefit as the children realize they are all in this together to make it work. This can lead to a mutual respect for and cooperation with the other decision-makers. The teacher can provide any necessary structure to support this collaborative attitude. She could say, for instance, "We will meet again on Monday afternoon after we play our new games to talk about any problems we find with indoor game play and figure out what we can do about each problem." Try some of the following action games during recess and see what happens in your classroom.

If your students are not used to game play, you might want to begin with a game that the whole class can play. As the children become more experienced with turn taking and collaboration, you can introduce some of the small group games for outdoor play. The game of BODY BINGO can be played in teams. Because of it's competitive nature, we found it well suited for third or fourth graders. It requires matrix game boards which can be drawn in chalk on the playground hardtop. The matrix game boards are configured according to the desired challenge or to your time constraints (e.g., matrix cells of 3x3, 4x4, or 5x5). Children (or the teacher) develop word problems. "Answers" are written on index cards and arranged one to each matrix cell. Children try answering questions prepared by the opposing team mates. If they answer the question successfully, they find the answer card and stand on that matrix cell until one team is able to get three (or four or five) players in a row on their game board. Eventually, the children learn strategies for arrangement of the answer cards, as well as a "batting order" for the players on their team. Other large group games you will want to try include NUMBER MARCH and NUMBER CATCH. Both of these are circle games which can be played at a variety of levels. For example, to play NUMBER MARCH with a missing addend challenge, children form a circle around an inner circle of giant playing cards. As the music plays, they march around this inner circle. When the music stops, the teacher calls out a number. The children pick up the card closest to them. The children look for someone holding a number card that, when added to their number card, will equal the number the teacher called. The teacher can continue to call the same number or for more difficulty, vary the numbers called. To play NUMBER CATCH, another circle game, the children catch a "problem" by looking to see where their thumbs are touching on a beach ball with one number written on each of the colored sections. To vary the difficulty, two-number addition, subtraction or multiplication versions can be played.

Remember the popular Milton Bradley game called Twister? Our version is NUMBER MIXER. It is played by placing number cards on the colored circles of the gameboard. Players are challenged not only to keep their balance but to try to be the first player to collect numbers which add to 20. Another game that the youngest children really enjoy playing is MONARCH OF THE MOUNTAIN. It

is a dice game which is played on a hopscotch-like track. Each player adds the roll of two dice to determine how far he or she can hop along the number track. When a player rolls a higher number than the previous player, that player is tagged out as he or she hops past. The tagged player skips around the number track and returns to the end of the line for another turn. The first player to get to the end is crowned MONARCH OF THE MOUNTAIN and reigns over the next round of play. The children loved the crown, cut out of oak tag board and embellished with craft store jewels and glitter. This was another very successful introductory game with a lot of action. It can be played by up to 10 children at one time.

All the games included in this chapter offer various thinking challenges to children and can be played outdoors. Outdoor game play may be just the right way to introduce math games to eager students who have not had a lot of experience with cooperative learning. Try out some "Thinking on Your Feet" with these games and see.

MONARCH OF THE MOUNTAIN

Good Game for: Counting, addition, addends from 1 to 6

Of Interest for Ages: 5-7 years   **Number of Players:** 4+

Materials Needed to Play: 1-12 number track game board, 2 dice, plastic bowl, crown

Make Your Own Materials: Follow the model to make a number track on bulletin board paper or go outside and draw one on the side walk with chalk. Help the children make the crown and decorate with craft-store "gems" and glitter.

Set-up to Play: Players line up at game board beside the number 1. Bowl is placed at start to catch the dice roll. The crown is placed on the game board at number 12.

Game Rules:
1. Order of play is determined by the roll of dice. Highest number goes first.
2. First player rolls the dice into the bowl and jumps on every number accordingly.
3. Next player rolls the dice. If sum is lower than the roll of the first or previous players, this player jumps on each number accordingly, and all players standing on higher numbers jump forward one space. If the number rolled is higher, this player jumps accordingly, but along the way, "tags" any passed players. The "tagged" players skip around the game board and return to start to begin again.
4. Play continues with previous players advancing one space when the sum of the roll is lower *or* being tagged when a player gets an equal or higher sum.
5. The first player to reach number 12 is "Monarch of the Mountain" and is "crowned." Players return to start line to begin again, as the Monarch looks on.

Object of the Game: To roll the highest number, jump to number 12 on the number track, and be crowned "Monarch of the Mountain."

Game Variations: The age of the players will dictate the complexity of the scoring. Younger children feel no need for scoring. Older children may want to award points for each round won. For example, we scored five points for each "crowning." The game was won when one player had a total of 25 points.

Game History: Adapted from an original game by Susan Gilles, kindergarten teacher at Harding Academy, Nashville, TN.

NUMBER CATCH

Good Game for: Addition, subtraction (multiplication)

Of Interest for Ages: 6-9 years   **Number of Players:** 9+

Materials Needed to Play: Inflatable, multi-colored beach ball, permanent marking pen

Make Your Own Materials: Inflate the beach ball and write one number in each of the colored sections of the ball with the marking pen. Underline the 6 and the 9 so players can tell which number is which if caught upside down. Some teachers prefer to include zero. Other teachers begin with one then add as many other numbers as there are sections. (Option: Two math operation signs (e.g., +, -, x) may be placed on the top and bottom of the ball.)

Set-up to Play: The players form a large circle so the beach ball can be thrown across the center to another player. It should be decided by the players ahead of time if it is exclusively an addition, subtraction, or multiplication game or if the math operation is also determined by the catch (see option in the above section).

Game Rules:
1. The teacher begins play by tossing the beach ball to a player in the circle.
2. The player who catches the ball looks to see what numbers are on the sections his or her two hands are touching. The player then must add, subtract or multiply these two numbers. If the math operation is also determined by catch, the player looks for the upward most of the two operation signs written on the ball. The player must perform that top most operation on the two numbers.

Object of the Game: To figure out the correct answer to the problem "caught."

Game Variations: Older children can play with multiplication or the "caught" operation described above. Sometimes older children will want to keep score and will devise a means to do this. This game works well as a team relay with a ball and a team leader for each team. The team leader throws the ball to a player on his or her team who gives the answer to the problem then throws the ball back to the team leader.

Game History: Adapted from a traditional classroom game by Sally Smyrl, 1st grade teacher at Achilles Elementary School in Gloucester County, VA.

BODY BINGO

Good Game for: Addition, subtraction, multiplication, or division

Of Interest for Ages: 6-9 years   **Number of Players:** 20+

Materials Needed to Play: 2 Body Bingo game boards, 50 number problem cards, marking pen, index cards, masking tape

Make Your Own Materials: Arrange carpet samples in two 5x5 matrices to make two game boards. The children can work in teams to make 25 number problems for the other team to figure out. Number problems are written on small index cards. Answers for the problems are written on large index cards.

Set-up to Play: Each team tapes the 25 answer cards (see above) to the 25 spaces of the opposing team's game board. Each team shuffles their problem cards.

Game Rules:
1. The teams line up and the first player of Team A reads the first number problem card to the first player of Team B.
2. If the first player of Team B can answer the problem correctly, he or she stands on the answer on his team's Bingo board. If not, the player goes to the end of the team line to await another turn. When the number problem card is not answered correctly, it is removed from the stack of cards for that game.
3. The play continues with players rotating forward until one team gets BINGO!

Object of the Game: To answer the questions correctly and to get five players in a row on your team's game board for BODY BINGO!

Game Variations: Younger children may prefer to play this game collaboratively rather than individually. (I.e., each team works together to figure out the answer, which is then given by the person at the head of that team's line. A Jeopardy-twist is added when answer cards are assigned by either the teacher or the other team and the number problems must be developed to fit those answers. Children who play this game often start arranging the answer cards strategically rather than randomly.

Game History: Adapted from a traditional classroom game by Anne Malsbury, Special Education teacher at Southeaster Elementary School in Chesapeake, VA.

$$$TEN BUCKS$$$

Good Game for: Making change, coin recognition, addition, doubling

Of Interest for Ages: 6-9 years   **Number of Players:** 2-4

Materials Needed to Play: 10 bowling pins with $ value labels, tennis ball, play money, money box "bank," number spinner

Make Your Own Materials: Make bowling pins out of one-liter soda bottles by filling insides with white latex paint. Drain excess paint and dry upside down. Replace bottle caps and add horizonal strips with colored tape. Look for old bowling pin games at yard sales. An excellent spinner can be made with a brass fastener and a giant paper clip. See illustration on page 203.

Set-up to Play: Place labels of different values on each of the ten bowling pins. (E.g., one pin can be labeled .01, another .05, another .10, another .15, .25, $1.00, etc.)

Game Rules:
1. Arrange the bowling pins in the traditional pyramid formation.
2. Use the spinner to determine order of play.
3. First player spins the spinner to get a number, then rolls the game ball toward the bowling pins. If the player knocks over the same number of pins as the number spun, the player's score is doubled. For example, if you spin a three and your ball knocks down three pins that are marked .01, .10 and 1.00, you would collect double $1.11 or $2.22 from the money box.

Object of the Game: To collect the most money from the bank. The first player to collect a total of Ten Bucks (i.e., $10) is the winner.

Game Variations: Young children may need coin stickers in addition to the decimal labels on the bowling pins. They can take from the bank those coins pictured on each pin they knock down. This game can be played without money by placing numbers from one to ten on the bowling pins. Players add the numbers on the fallen pins to determine their score. Very young children can simply count the fallen pins.

Game History: Adapted from an original game by Sonya Hendren, lead teacher in the two-year-old room at the Old Dominion University Child Development Center, Norfolk, VA.

NUMBER MARCH

Good Game for: Early addition, addends 4 through 10

Of Interest for Ages: 5-7 years   **Number of Players:** 5+

Materials Needed to Play: 1 or 2 decks of giant-size playing cards

Make Your Own Materials: The plastic-coated, giant playing cards available through school stores and catalogs work very well for this game. Make your own giant playing cards by modeling them after the counting cards used in previous game.

Set-up to Play: The leader shuffles the cards to be used from one to two decks (e.g., four or eight cards each of numbers one to four). Place the cards randomly on the floor in a large circle with one number card placed for each child playing.

Game Rules:
1. Children march around the outside of the circle of cards while singing (to the tune of <u>Mary Had a Little Lamb</u>):

   Marching 'round the number wheel, Number wheel, number wheel.
   Marching 'round the number wheel, Now let's make a "____" (Leader calls out number.)

2. When the song ends, the children stop and pick up the nearest number card, then look for another child holding a number needed to total the number called out.
3. All children may not find the number they need. (E.g., If a FIVE is called, each child with a number one must find a child with a number four to total five).
4. Children who find another child with the number they need may keep their cards. Other children must return their cards to the circle. The leader fills in the gaps with the remaining number cards. Play continues until all cards have been paired.

Object of the Game: To have the most cards at the end of the game.

Game Variations: Start with small groups and addends up to four. Increase size of the group and the numbers, as children experience success and are ready for further challenge. Very young children enjoy matching their numbers.

Game History: Adapted from an original game by Marian Hernandez, preschool teacher at All Saints' Day School in Virginia Beach, VA.

NUMBER MIXER

Good Game for: Addition, mental math, (multiplication, subtraction)

Of Interest for Ages: 6-9 years   **Number of Players:** 3

Materials Needed to Play: 4x6 foot game board, spinner, number cards, masking tape

Make Your Own Materials: We used a Twister game board and taped a number to each circle, but you can make your own game board using poster board circles on a plastic table cloth. Make your own spinner with a brass fastener and a giant paper clip.

Set-up to Play: Spread the game board out on the floor with a number card taped to each circle. Equal low numbers (or zeros) should be on the blue and yellow starting circles. Players need to take off their shoes so the playing board is not damaged.

Game Rules:
1. Three players spin to detemine order of play. The players who spin the highest and second highest numbers go first and second; third is the caller. Play rotates after the first round, when first player becomes caller and caller takes second player's position, etc. Players one and two take their positions facing one another at opposite ends of board, each standing on the closest yellow and blue circles.
2. The caller spins the spinner and calls out the color and body part. The first player chooses body placement considering balance but trying for the highest numbers. The caller spins again and the second player moves accordingly.
3. Play alternates between the two players, and points are added for each move. Round of play ends when one player loses balance, giving the opponent 5 points.
4. Players rotate positions at the end of each round, and play continues until one player accumulates 20 points (or more).

Object of the Game: To keep your balance and be the first to reach game point goal.

Game Variations: This game can be played with teams. If addition is too easy, subtract the numbers from 20. Multiplication is a good variation for older children.

Game History: Inspired by Twister, a Milton Bradley game, and adapted from an original version by Rebecca Lynn Anderson, teacher-in-training at Old Dominion University, Norfolk, VA.

CHAPTER 6

INTEGRATING LANGUAGE ARTS

"...the younger the children, the more informal and integrated the curriculum should be."
                                                              - Lilian Katz (1989, p. 49)

Usually teachers of young children recognize the value of integrating subjects across the school curriculum. Many adults remember the disjointed change from one academic area to the next when they were in elementary school. As we teachers gain a better understanding for how learning occurs, we are improving ways to present academic knowledge to our students. Gradually, we are developing instructional strategies that work with rather than against the learning process. For example, we understand that we humans are meaning-makers. Teachers and parents who recognize the implication of this regularly put children in the position of figuring things out for themselves (i.e., making meaning). This learning process is disrupted when the teacher stops the process because it is time for the next subject or lunch or recess. When subjects are integrated across the curriculum, the thinking is more likely to continue.

Stories are a natural connection between math and language arts. Some stories quite obviously deal with number. For example, Judith Viorst's <u>Alexander Who used to be Rich Last Sunday</u> is a favorite for encouraging children to think about money. There are many others. However, teachers can connect almost any story with math simply by making a board game which requires players to add dice, move game markers, and/or follow chance card instructions according to the story line. <u>The Rainbow Fish</u> by Marcus Pfiste is a good example. The theme of this story is friendship and sharing. The connection between this story and math thinking occurs while rolling a die (i.e., number recognition), moving a marker around the game board (i.e., counting) and giving away all but one of the player's shiny fish scales (i.e., subtracting). The story themes of friendship and sharing integrate social studies and reading into this math activity.

The games in this chapter are related to some favorite children's stories. For the most part, these stories are told in picture books which the children return to again and again to enjoy after their first encounter. We have observed this same pattern of repeated return when children are introduced to a favorite story game.

The exception to the usual picture book format is Robert Louis Stevenson's classic story, Treasure Island. This gripping adventure is more appropriate to read to 3rd and 4th graders. However, our Treasure Island Game was also a favorite with very young children who loved collecting craft-store "jewels" to put in their treasure chests. Another popular story and game for the youngest children is Eric Carle's story, The Very Hungry Caterpillar. A variation of this game also appealed to older children who subtracted their dice roll to determine their move. Although the older children remembered the story fondly, they were generally more interested in playing the game than in reading the story again. Although we got better at predicting the children's responses to the various games, we were regularly surprised too.

MONKEYS IN THE TREE was based on a counting rhyme by Kelly Oechsli called Two Many Monkeys! It reminded me of "Hi Ho, Cherrio" which my children enjoyed playing. Instead of collecting cherries from the tree, this game had monkeys in the tree. Children tried to get them off before their spinner pointed to the spilled bananas and all the monkeys had to be put back on the tree. Each child was taking off (i.e.,

subtracting) and putting back (i.e., adding) 10 monkeys during this game. By adding ten hats to the ten monkeys, we thought this game could be played to extend Esphyr Slovodkina's wonderful story, Caps for Sale.

Since subtraction is such a mental stretch for children to make, I am always on the alert for games to gently nudge children in that direction. Another game which requires the players to consider differences is based on a picture book I wrote called Those Calculating Crows. This game is similar to Parcheesi in that each player has multiple playing pieces to move to a "home" base on the other side of the game board. Players have to consider which game piece to move and whether to move one piece the total roll, or two pieces according to each die. To avoid hazards and reach home, the children must figure out the best use of their dice roll. There is plenty of thinking as players try to keep track of their own pieces, as well as those of the other players.

Many of these games can be adapted for a multiplication challenge simply by using one die which is rolled then multiplied by a constant number. The response of children to multiplying their die roll by two was interesting to watch. Teachers who teach children to multiply by memorizing their times tables ought to observe children play games this way. As the children figured out multiples of their roll by using their natural ability to think, we learned about the various ways children construct multiplicative thinking. The way most children make sense of multiplication is by repeated addition. Game play such as this allows for children to experiment with doubling or "times 2" as they construct the meaning of this idea.

One parent I know was so upset about her daughter's homework assignment in second grade. The daughter had been told to memorize the three times tables for the next day. The parent tried to help her daughter understand what "three times" meant, but the daughter was unable to comprehend any underlying meaning. She kept repeating that she had to know it by tomorrow. We all recognize how difficult it is to memorize something that has no meaning. There were tears shed over that assignment in more than one household that night. The sad thing is that tears are *never* necessary to learn and do something that is fun and meaningful. Games can be both!

THE VERY HUNGRY CATERPILLAR

Good Game for: counting, number recognition, (subtraction)

Of Interest for Ages: 4-6 years   **Number of Players:** 2-4

Materials Needed to Play: Game board, 4 caterpillar markers, 4 butterflies, 4 "growing" caterpillars, pom poms, "cocoon," spinner

Make Your Own Materials: Remove, assemble, color and laminate the game board. Game markers can be made out of colored chenille pipe cleaners. We made the body to our "growing" caterpillars by gluing velcro on two tongue depressors laid end-to-end. A head was fashioned by gluing wiggle eyes onto a pom pom glued to one end of the velco strip body. A brown paper lunch bag served as a "cocoon."

Set-up to Play: Each player needs a caterpiller marker and a "growing" caterpillar. The butterflies should be placed in the "cocoon" paper bag.

Game Rules:
1. Player spin to determine order of play.
2. Players spin the spinner and move accordingly. When landing on food picture, the player takes pom pom(s) to represent what the caterpillar ate (e.g., 3 strawberries = 3 pom poms). When landing on "sick" caterpillar, player puts back a pom pom because the caterpillar ate too much.
3. When player comes to end of game board, caterpillar marker is placed inside the "cocoon." On next turn, the player removes beautiful butterfly from the "cocoon."
4. When first player finishes, all pom poms removed due to landing on "sick" caterpillar go to this first finisher.
5. Whoever has the most pom poms after all players claim their butterflies wins.

Object of the Game: To have the most pom poms after all players have finished game.

Game Variations: Older children can subtract roll of two dice to determine move.

Game History: Inspired by Eric Carle's story, <u>The Very Hungry Caterpiller</u>, and adapted from an original game by Susan Gilles, kindergarten teacher at Harding Academy, Nashville, TN.

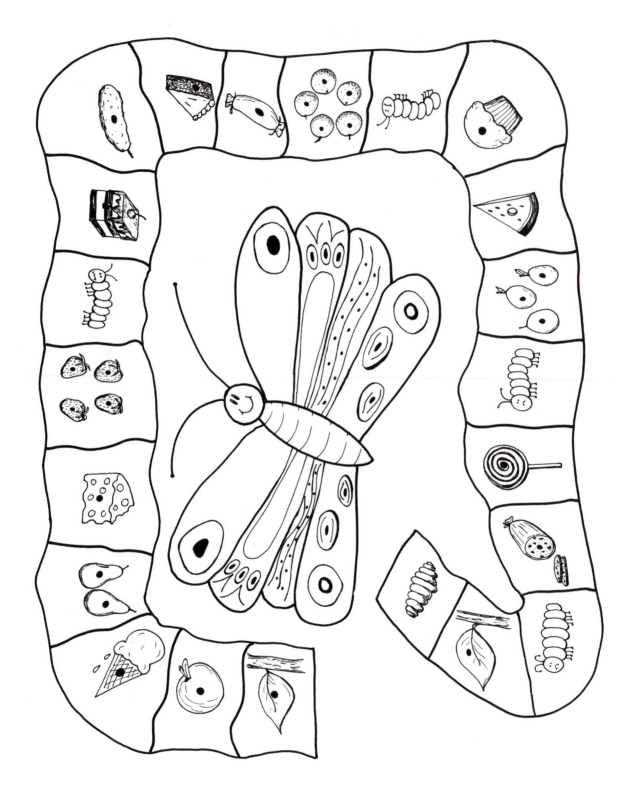

The gameboard should look like this when assembled.

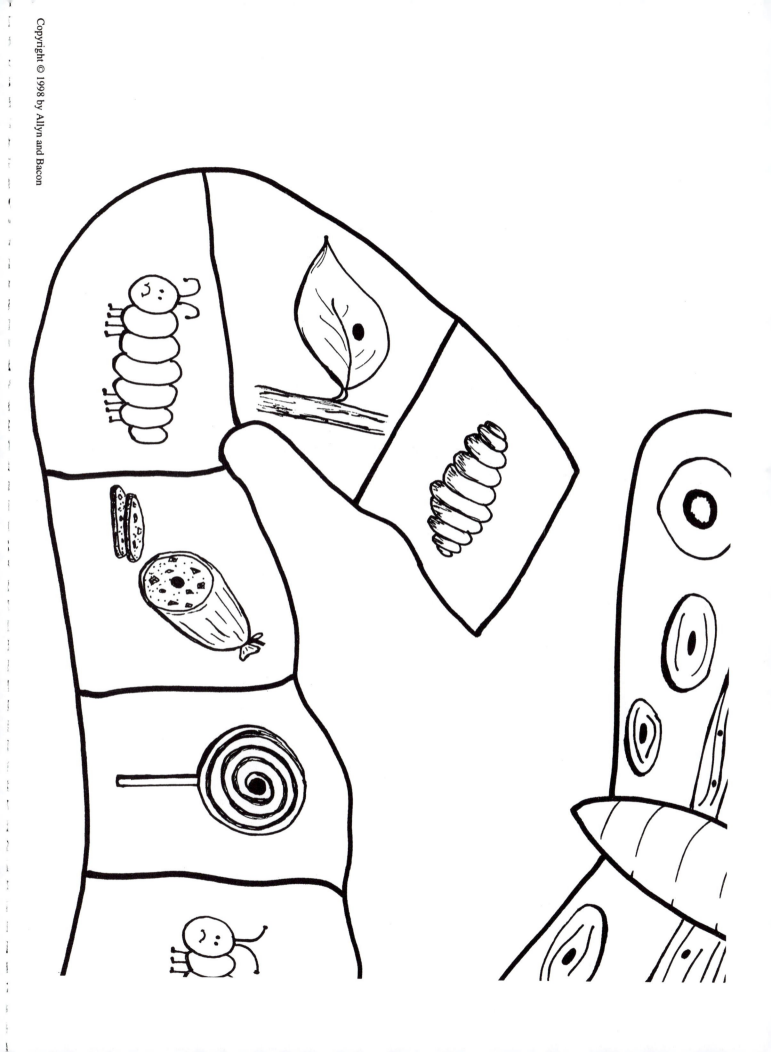

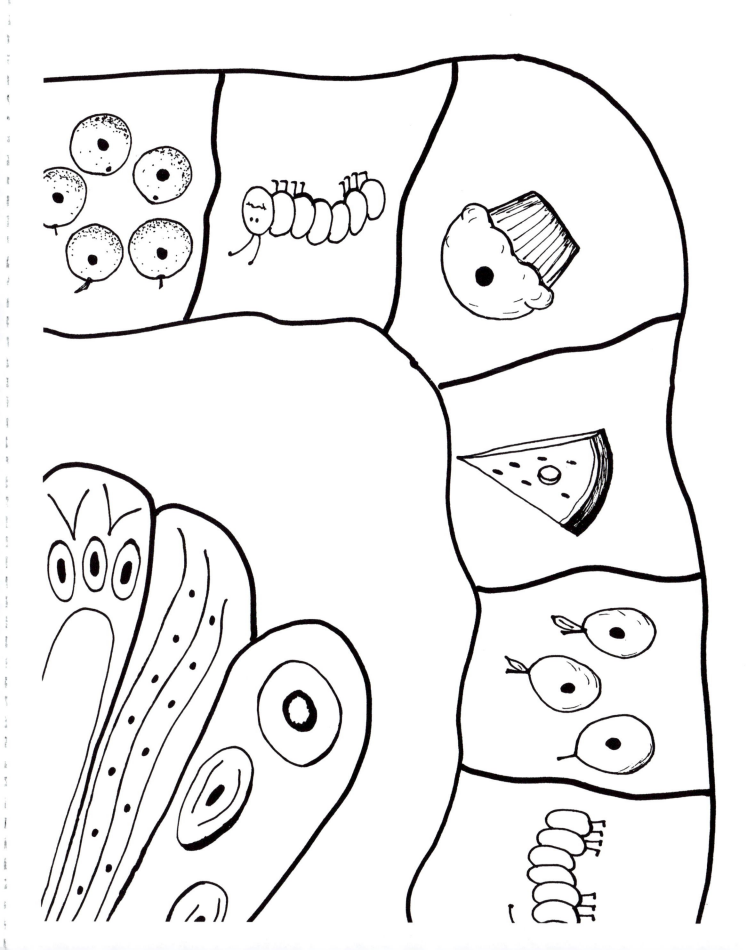

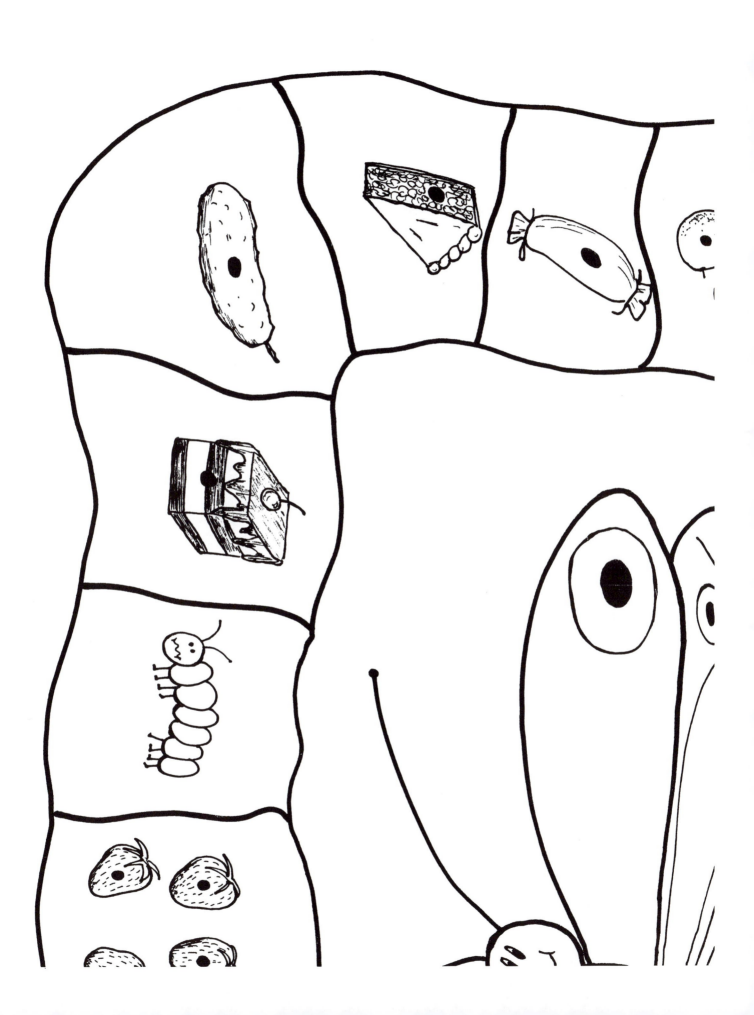

THE RAINBOW FISH

Good Game for: number recognition, counting, differences of 1 (addition, subtraction)

Of Interest for Ages: 5-7 years   **Number of Players:** 2-4

Materials Needed to Play: Game board, 4 game markers, 4 rainbow fish, 45 shiny fish "scales," 1 die or number spinner

Make Your Own Materials: Carefully remove and assemble the four sections of the game board. Color and laminate. We used fish erasers for our game markers but dry lima beans work as well. The Rainbow Fish can be modeled after the one in the book and cut out of different colors of poster board. The fish "scales" can be made from one inch circles of the shimmering wrapping paper or cloth which looks similar to the scales in the book. To last longer, the scales should be laminated.

Set-up to Play: To begin the game, each player picks a game marker and a Rainbow Fish. Each player places ten shimmering "scales" on his or her fish.

Game Rules:
1. Use spinner (or die) to determine order of play.
2. The player spins the spinner (or rolls die) to see how many spaces to move game marker. If the player lands on an octopus, he or she must place one of his or her shimmering scales on a fish in the center of the game board.
3. Play continues around the gameboard until one player has only one shimmering scale left on his rainbow fish. That player is the winner.

Object of the Game: To give away all but one of your shimmering scales.

Game Variations: Older children can play with two dice which are added or subtracted to determine the move. For very young children, you might want to start the game with five scales instead of ten.

Game History: Inspired by Marcus Pfiste's story, The Rainbow Fish, and adapted from an original game by Deirdre J. Dean, Director at All Saints' Day School in Virginia Beach, VA.

The gameboard should look like this when assembled.

TREASURE ISLAND

Good Game for: "putting on" (i.e., addition), "taking off" (i.e., subtraction), number recognition, counting

Of Interest for Ages: 5-7 years   **Number of Players:** 2-4

Materials Needed to Play: Game board, 4 game markers, 4 game "treasure chest" grids, box of "jewels," 1 die

Make Your Own Materials: Carefully remove, assemble, color and laminate the game board. The "treasure chests" are made by making a one-inch grid on different colors of poster board or felt. Look for the "jewels" at your local craft store. We found pirate hats for the game markers but buttons work fine.

Set-up to Play: Each player needs a game marker and a "treasure chest" grid.

Game Rules:
1. Use die to determine order of play. The roll of die by the last player of this opening round determines the number of "jewels" in the bonus cache placed on the game board ship which is collected by the first player to reach the pirate ship.
2. Each player rolls the die and moves his or her game marker accordingly. Whenever a player lands on a space with a treasure chest, a roll of the die determines how many jewels can be claimed and placed on his "treasure chest" grid. If the player lands on a pirate flag, a roll of the die determines how many "jewels" must be removed from the player's grid and put back into the game box.
3. Players may take short cuts to the ship but risk passing more pirate flags this way.
4. Play continues around the board toward the ship until all players reach the ship. Only the first player to reach the ship claims the bonus "jewels."
6. The player with the most "jewels" is the winner.

Object of the Game: To collect the most "jewels" by the time all players finish.

Game Variations: Older children can subtract dice roll to determine their move. Older children like to roll the exact number to board the ship at the end of the game.

Game History: Inspired by Robert Louis Stevenson's classic story, <u>Treasure Island</u>, and adapted from an original game by Deirdre J. Dean, Director at All Saints' Day School in Virginia Beach, VA

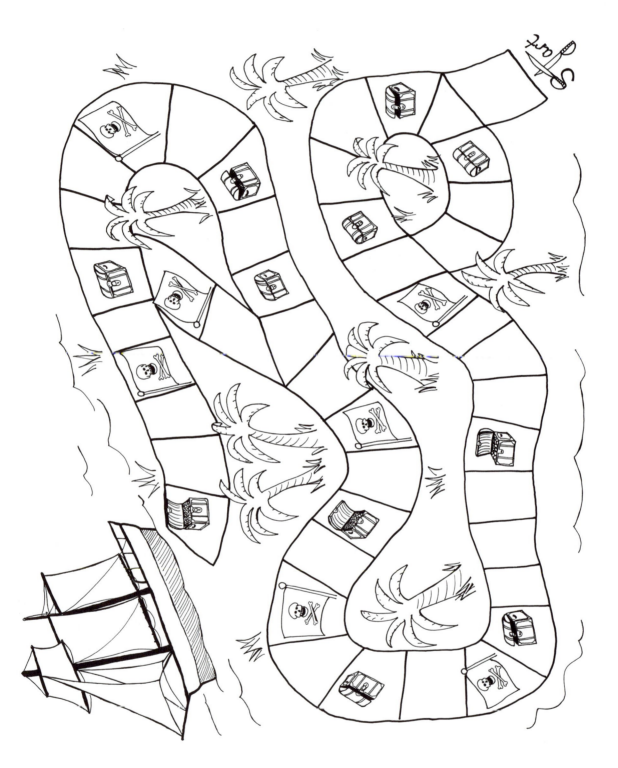

Start

The gameboard should look like this when assembled.

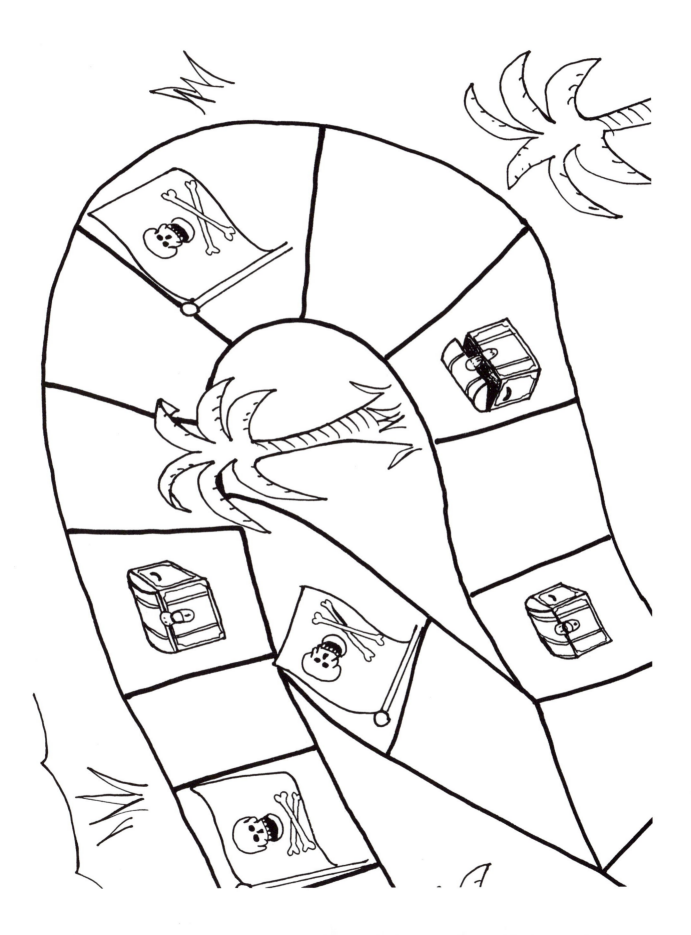

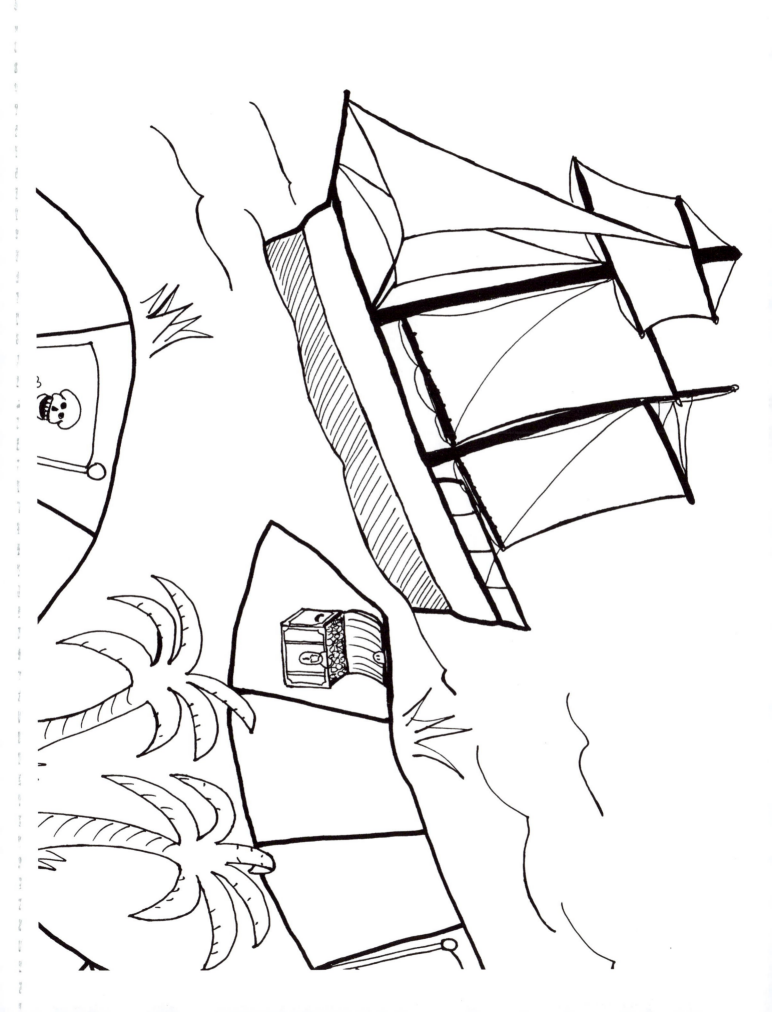

MONKEYS IN THE TREE

Good Game for: "putting on" (i.e., addition), "taking off" (i.e., subtraction), number recognition, counting

Of Interest for Ages: 5-7 years   **Number of Players:** 2-4

Materials Needed to Play: 4 tree game boards, 4 berry baskets, 40 monkeys cards, (and hats), monkey spinner (or dice)

Make Your Own Materials: Carefully remove, color and laminate the 4 tree game boards. Lattice berry baskets make excellent playing baskets. The 40 monkeys cards are colored, laminated and cut apart. Attach spinner to spinner dial provided.

Set-up to Play: To begin the game, the players each take a berry basket and a tree game board and place 10 monkeys cards on their tree.

Game Rules:
1. Use spinner (or die) to determine order of play.
2. The player spins the monkey spinner (or rolls dice). If the spinner points to monkeys, that number of monkey cards are removed from his or her tree and placed into the player's basket. If the spinner points to the bees or tire swing, the player must remove two monkeys from his or her basket and replace them on the tree. If the spinner points to the spilled bananas, the player must put all his or her monkeys back on the tree and start over.
3. Play continues until one player has all ten monkeys in his or her basket to win.

Object of the Game: To collect all ten monkeys from your tree.

Game Variations: Older children can play with two dice which are subtracted to determine number of monkeys that may be removed from the tree. The hazards of bees, tire swing and spilled bananas can be drawn on dot stickers and placed on the sides of one of the die. Forty hats can be added to the 40 monkeys and a longer version of the game can be played as a follow-up to the classic children's story of Caps for Sale by Esphyr Slovodkina.

Game History: Inspired by Kelly Oechsli's counting rhyme, Two Many Monkeys! and adapted from an original game by Nancy Eason, Pre-K teacher at Mary Peake Early Childhood Center, Hampton, VA.

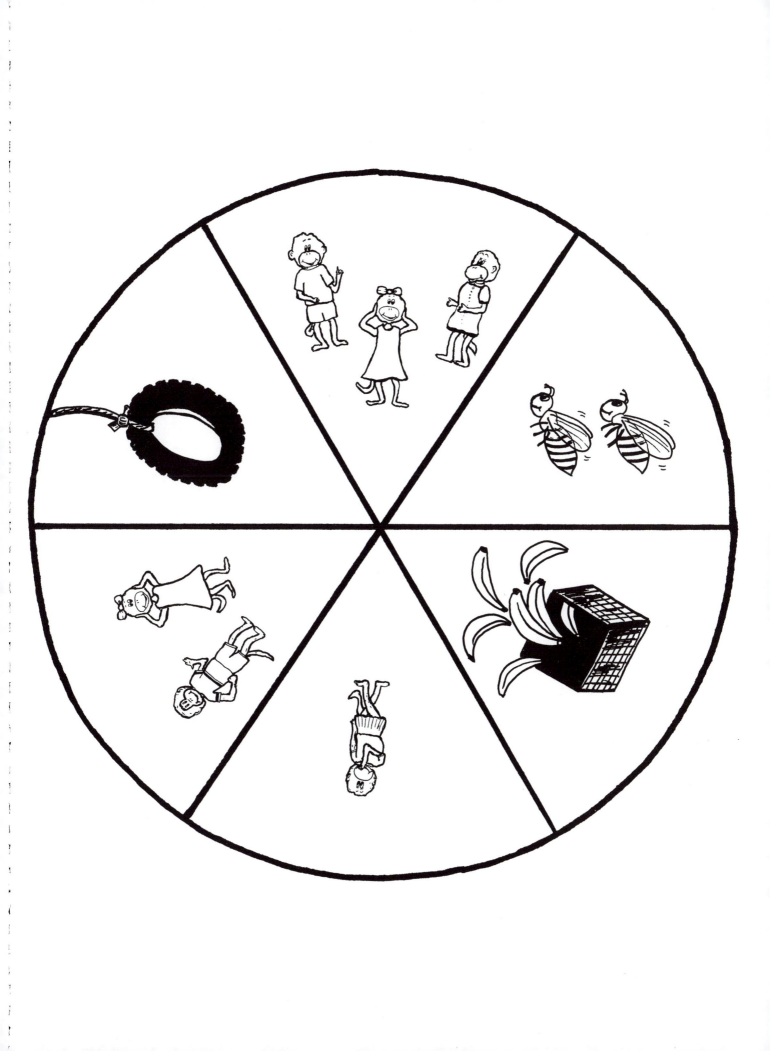

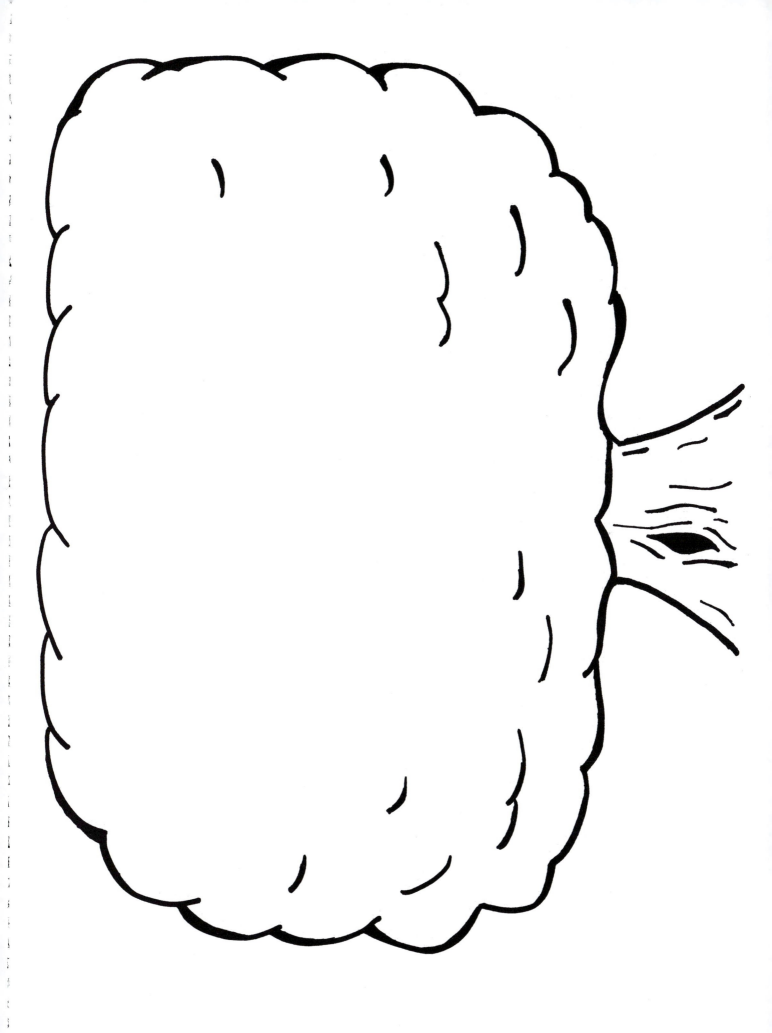

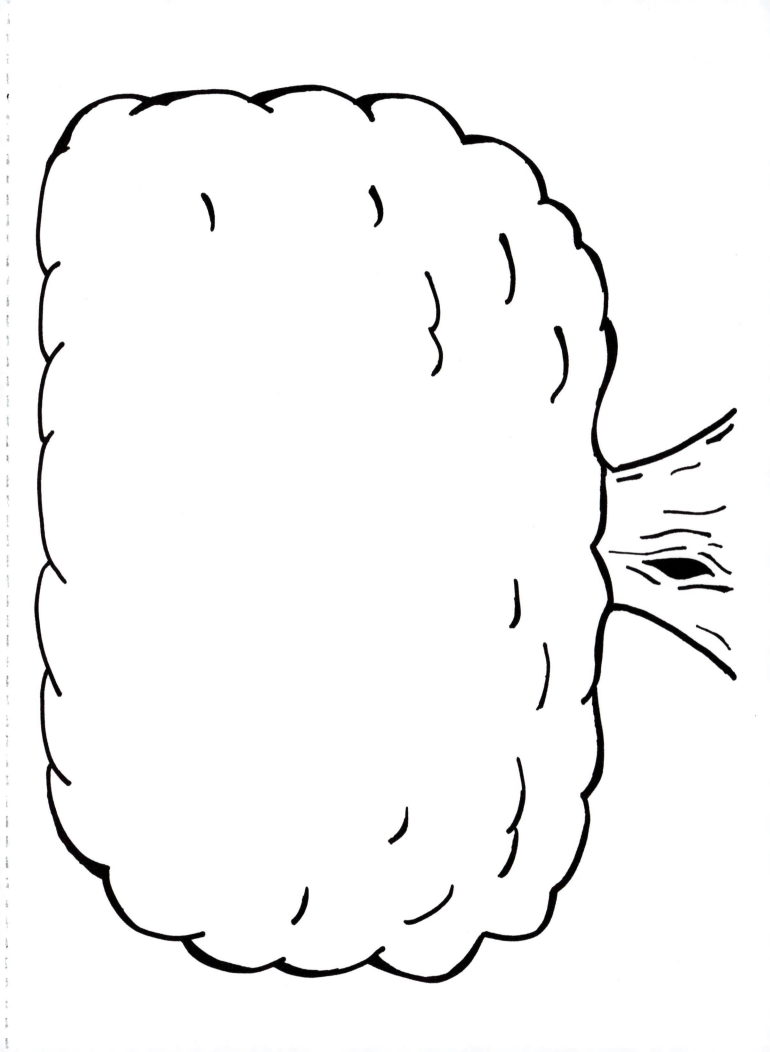

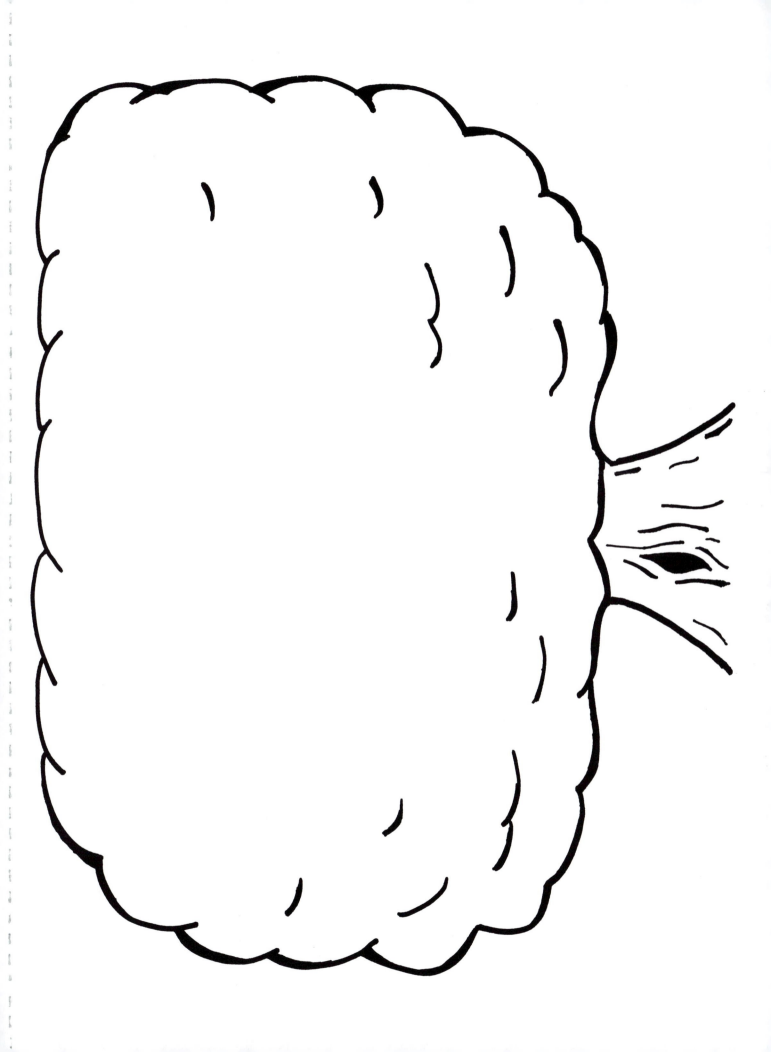

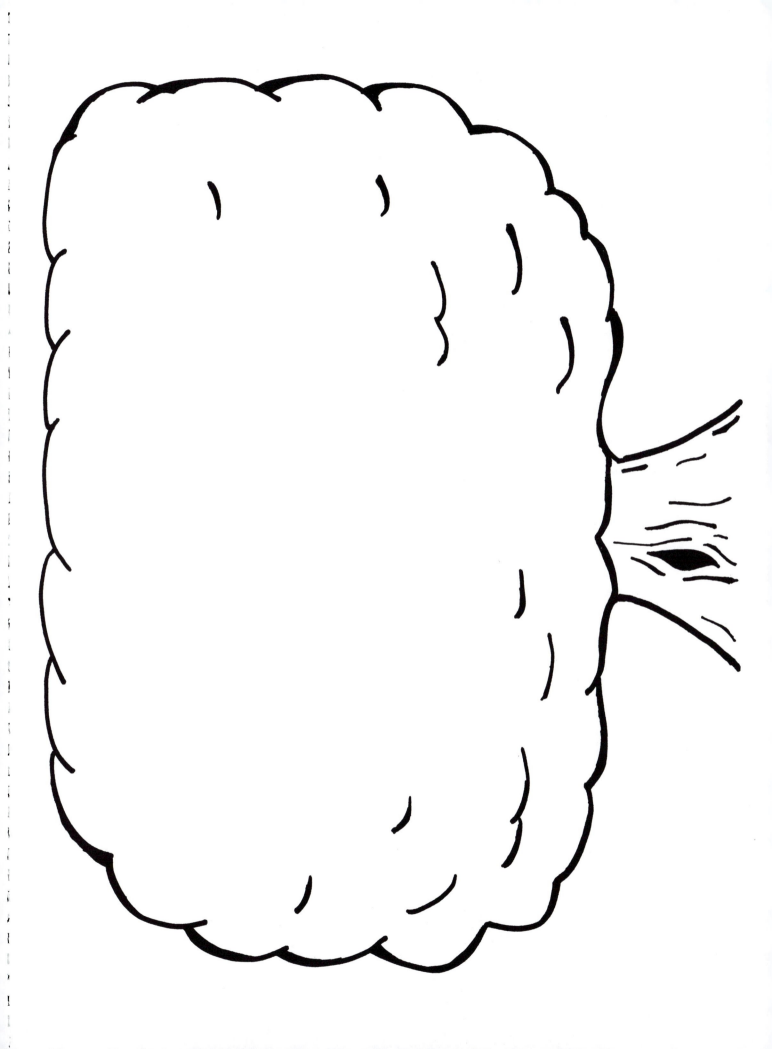

Eight Monkey

Cards

of 40-card Deck

Eight Monkey

Cards

of 40-card Deck

Eight Monkey

Cards

of 40-card Deck

Eight Monkey

Cards

of 40-card Deck

Eight-Monkey

Cards

of 40-card Deck

THOSE CALCULATING CROWS

Good Game for: Addition, counting and subtraction (doubling)

Of Interest for Ages: 6-9 years   **Number of Players:** 2-4

Materials Needed to Play: Game board, 8 game markers for each player, 2 dice brass fastener (optional)

Make Your Own Materials: Color and laminate the four game boards. The game boards may be connected by punching holes in the upper right hand corners and incerting a brass fastener. Fan them open to play. We used 4 colors of spray-painted lima beans as the game markers.

Set-up to Play: Each player takes 8 game markers of the same color and lines them up on top of the circles on the left side of the game board.

Game Rules:
1. Use dice to determine order of play. Play rotates clockwise from player to player.
2. Each player rolls dice, adds the roll to move one game marker or uses each die separately to move two game markers toward the garden shed. If the player lands on an ear of corn, he or she receives an extra turn. If the player lands on a crow track, then he or she must go back one space.
3. Play continues until one player gets all eight of his or her game markers through the garden shed and down the path to cover the eight numbers at the bottom of the game board.

Object of the Game: To travel along the game board path and be the first player to get all eight game markers onto numbers one to eight at the bottom of the game board.

Game Variations: This game requires players to think about the consequences of which game marker to use and whether there is an advantage to move one or two markers. Doubling could be emphasized by using one die which is doubled (or multiplied by two) when rolled.

Game History: Inspired by Ali Wakefield's story, Those Calculating Crows, and adapted from an original game by Courtney Waterfield Saintsing at John B. Dey Elementary School in Virginia Beach, VA.

1   2   3   4   5   6   7   8

1 2 3 4 5 6 7 8

1 2 3 4 5 6 7 8

1   2   3   4   5   6   7   8

CHAPTER 7

ON BEYOND GAMES

"What you do about what you don't know is, in the final analysis, what determines what you will ultimately know."

- Eleanor Duckworth (1987, p. 68)

In Chapter Two, I discussed the irony of asking children to do worksheets to learn their number "facts." If children already know these number relationships, the worksheet is, at best, unnecessary busy work. For the children who have not yet formed these number relationships, a worksheet offers little incentive for figuring them out. For these children, the worksheet may simply serve as a daily reminder of how little they know about math.

There is yet another harmful aspect to worksheets that must be addressed. If children, both those who know their number relationships and those who do not, are only presented with problems written out in equation-form, they never have the opportunity to figure out for themselves what the problem is. Since problem-finding is only constructed by finding problems, it should not be surprising that children who are never put in the position of doing this are not likely to construct the ability to do it.

So, besides the obvious, to avoid practice work sheets, what is a teacher to do? First, let us consider whether problem-finding can be taught directly. Do you remember how difficult story or word problems were in upper elementary school? If you have that recollection, as I do, think back. Do you recall directions from the teacher on how to "find the problem?" Always wanting to be helpful, teachers still direct their students to look for "clue words" to indicate how to set up the problem. For example, the words "and" and "difference" are clues for addition and subtraction. On the surface, that would seem to be a useful strategy to share with children. However, when children isolate "clue" words from the sense of the whole problem, the result is apt to be nonsense. The following account is a poignant example of this. In the study by Kamii and Lewis (1991) which was referred to in Chapter One, the researchers compared second graders who had been taught by constructivist

---

teachers with those taught by traditional teachers. The constructivist teachers based their math instruction on the premise that children must be meaningfully engaged (i.e, thinking) to form math logic. Children in these classes did not get isolated lessons on how to get right answers, but rather were given many opportunities to form number relationships and confront number problems from a "need-to-know" perspective. Children in the traditional classes were taught with traditional methods including memorized algorithms and practice problems. The two groups both did well at "finding right answers," as determined by normed achievement tests. However, when the children were asked to solve math "word" problems in one-on-one interviews, some interesting differences between the two groups became apparent. One of the questions the children were asked was, "if there are 26 sheep and 10 goats on a ship, how old is the captain of the ship?" Twenty-seven percent of the constructivist-taught second-grade children said the question did not make sense. None of the traditionally-taught children were disturbed by this nonsensical question.

When traditional teachers hear that their students may be asked such a question, their typical response is to add new math skill objectives to their lesson plans on how to determine if a problem makes sense! Constructivist teachers take a very different approach. They recognize that the key to "teaching" how to determine if a problem makes sense is to give children "real life" problems and ask the children to make sense of them. For example, children can be asked how many tables should be ordered for the new classroom, if 4 children can sit at each table, and there are 28 children in the class. Constructivist teachers let the children struggle with problems such as this in a way that makes sense to them. The children do not have to find "clue" words and set up a division equation to solve this problem. Children will tackle this problem based on what makes sense to them. For example, some children will pull fours until they add up to 28, then count how many were needed. Other children may start with 28 and subtract fours until there are no children left and then count how many fours were needed to determine the number of tables required. Some children think best by drawing tables then "placing" four children around each table until 28 children are "seated." Some children may only watch the other children as they figure it out. These children may be building a bridge to figuring out the next problem more independently. Children who make sense of problems based on what they know will eventually learn to recognize the difference between sense and nonsense. Teaching a "skill" in isolation from the overall meaning is more likely to be mind-boggling than mind-engaging. Thinkers, experienced and inexperienced alike, are not inclined to make sense of their world in this manner.

By now you may be getting the distinct impression that no matter how good a teacher may be, he or she can not directly tell another person how to form a logico-mathematical operation, nor is that operation formed by rote practice. So what can a teacher do to encourage math logic? Instead of direct teaching, we must put our students in situations in which they must figure out both the problem and the solution for themselves. And, instead of rote practice, we must find activities that allow for repeated but meaningful mental engagement. If teachers can do this, their students will be far more liable to construct math logic. If teachers can do this and understand WHY it is beneficial, they are on their way to becoming constructivist teachers.

My experience has been that the application of constructivism is not that difficult for most teachers. The most difficult part for teachers is the construction of constructivism in the first place. It is much harder for teachers to explain why allowing children to figure out the answers for themselves is more beneficial than telling or even showing children how to find the answer. Just as children construct an understanding for counting or multiplicative thinking, teachers construct an understanding for how math learning occurs. Their math teaching is simply the reflection of that understanding.

Constructing an understanding for how math learning occurs is not easy. We are all aware of some of the hurdles.

For example, we are obviously influenced by the math programs published by big publishing houses and by the math objectives that come out of our central offices and state departments. We remember how we were taught math. We see how other teachers are teaching math. Actually, there can be a lot to overcome. However, it is *not* impossible. Once you begin to think about constructing math logic, and begin to investigate, you will find some compelling evidence. You, just as the children, will build on your previous knowledge base and move toward a more complex understanding. God speed to us all!

Afterword

Throughout this book I have described classrooms designed with consideration for how young children construct their own math logic by forming math relationships for themselves. These constructivist classrooms tend to be environments in which teachers and children alike have and make choices, dare to take intellectual risks, and genuinely enjoy learning something new. Sadly, the reality for many classroom teachers is that they are not hired to make choices, take risks or model the thrill of learning. They are hired to ensure that the state and local objectives for the children in their classes are met.

Sometimes these objectives are not written with an understanding for the way we know that knowledge is constructed by children. For example, math objectives may specify that kindergarten children tell time "on the hour," and that first graders tell time to the "half hours." In second grade, "quarter hours" are added. This arbitrary sequence for learning how to measure time may only make sense to someone who already has a clear understanding for time in the first place. However, a typical kindergartner who is still confused about "yesterday, today and tomorrow," is incapable of figuring out how "something called time" is measured at *all*, let alone in such a meaningless progression.

Teachers and school administrators need to think about the long-term consequences of expecting children to memorize answers to questions that do not make sense to them. What goals do we have for our children anyway? Is it just the year-by-year objectives to read and write and compute? We recognize quickly that these objectives are not enough when school children learn to read but have no interest in reading after school. Likewise, what good is it, if school children only learn to do math problems by memorizing steps in a society that values critical thinking, problem solving and inventiveness? What good is it, if children are only well behaved and considerate in the presence of an authority figure? Obviously, we need long-term goals to guide us when trying to achieve our year-to-year objectives.

Ask educators or parents of young children what it is that they would wish for their students and children. It is surprising how similar the lists of aspirations are for both groups. Parents and teachers alike hope their children will be open to knowing about their world. They hope their children will be creative, self-reliant, self-governing, have initiative and confidence in their own ability as critical thinkers and problem solvers and that they will be sensitive to and get along with others. The very least we can expect from the school's short-term objectives is that they don't make achieving these long-term goals improbable. The following math objectives work well with our long-term goals for young children and have been useful to constructivist teachers I know who encourage their students to be math thinkers.

K-3 Arithmetic Objectives

Cognitive Objectives - Young children will:
    1. solve math problems by figuring them out
        without dependence upon paper, pencil,
        or memorized rules;
    2. solve math problems that they have not
        encountered before;
    3. explain through logic how a problem was
        solved;
    4. invent many different ways to solve the
        same problem;
    5. solve "word problems" involving numbers
        from their daily life;

Socio-cognitive Objectives - Young children will:
    6. exchange ideas in class discussions;
    7. correct their own logic in class
        discussions, as well as respectfully
        correct the logic of their classmates;

Affective Objectives - Young children will:
    8. develop their "number sense" (i.e.,
        intuition for knowing what is a
        reasonable answer);
    9. build math confidence and enthusiasm, as
        math competence is constructed.

There is one last question that I would direct to school administrators. How can we hope to fulfill long-term objectives for children to be curious, creative, self-reliant, self-governing, have initiative and confidence in their own ability to figure things out (Kamii & DeVries, 1980), if the same qualities are not expected from the teachers of those children? In spite of the limited control many teachers seem to have over what goes on in their classrooms, it is remarkable that so many of them think about how to determine and appropriately meet the needs of their young students. How can we support these teachers and encourage them to be educational problem solvers? If we are serious about improving the quality of our schools, it may be necessary to consider implementing long-term goals for teachers similar to those we would wish for their young students.

References

Burns, M. (1994). Arithmetic: The last holdout. <u>Phi Delta Kappan</u>, <u>75</u>(6), 471-47.

Duckworth, E. (1987). <u>The having of wonderful ideas and other essays on teaching and learning</u>. New York: Teachers College Press.

Kamii, C. K. (1985). <u>Young Children reinvent arithmetic:Implications of Piaget's theory</u>. New York: Teachers College Press.

Kamii, C. K. (1989). <u>Young Children continue to reinvent arithmetic:2nd grade</u>. New York: Teachers College Press.

Kamii, C. K. (1994). <u>Young Children continue to reinvent arithmetic:3rd grade</u>. New York: Teachers College Press.

Kamii, C., & DeVries, R. (1980). <u>Group games in early education</u>. Washington, DC: National Association for the Education of Young Children.

Kamii, C., & Lewis, B. A. (1991). Achievement tests in primary mathematics: Perpetuating lower-order thinking. <u>Arithmetic Teacher</u>, <u>38</u>(May), 4-9.

Katz, L. G, & Chard, S. C. (1989). <u>Engaging children's minds: The project approach</u>. Norwood, NJ: Ablex Publishing Corporation.

Leinwand, S. (1994, February 9). It's time to abandon computational algorithms. <u>Education Week</u>, p. 36.

Narode, R., Board, J., & Davenport, L. (1993). In J. R. Becker & B. J. Pence, (Eds.), Proceedings of the fifteenth annual meeting: North American Chapter of the

International Group for the Psychology of Mathematics Education, Vol. I.

Pacific Groves, CA: North American Chapter of the International Group for the

Psychology of Mathematics Education.

National Council of Teachers of Mathematics. (1989). Curriculum and evaluation

standards for school mathematics. Reston, VA: The Council.

Index